Sikh Children in Br...

Sikh Children in Britain

ALAN G. JAMES

Published for the
Institute of Race Relations, London
by
OXFORD UNIVERSITY PRESS
LONDON NEW YORK DELHI
1974

Oxford University Press, Ely House, London W. 1

GLASGOW NEW YORK TORONTO MELBOURNE WELLINGTON
CAPE TOWN IBADAN NAIROBI DAR ES SALAAM LUSAKA ADDIS ABABA
DELHI BOMBAY CALCUTTA MADRAS KARACHI LAHORE DACCA
KUALA LUMPUR SINGAPORE HONG KONG TOKYO

ISBN 0 19 218409 1

*Printed in Great Britain by
Northumberland Press Limited, Gateshead*

Contents

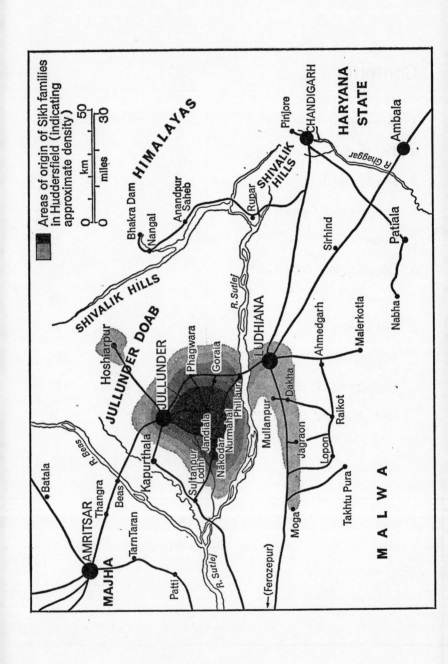

Areas of origin of Sikh families in Huddersfield (indicating approximate density)

1 Introduction

> The love and generosity of these Sikhs
> Have enriched my heart and my home
> *(Hazare Sabad* MX)[1]

My own life has been enriched by contact and involvement with the particular Sikh community that is the subject of this essay, since 1966 when I was appointed to teach at a Primary School in Huddersfield, with special responsibility for a class of newly arrived immigrant children. At that time, most of the children in this school were of immigrant parentage, and the majority were recent arrivals from overseas—from the Caribbean, from Pakistan, and from India. Amongst the, initially, non-English-speaking children in my class were several Sikhs. As time went on, I got to know these children and their parents very well, and became very friendly with increasing numbers of Sikhs in the neighbourhood. Their relaxed and unassuming hospitality helped me to obtain the kind of understanding of their way of life that I felt I needed, both in order to carry out my duties as a teacher, and to satisfy a real and growing personal interest. This sort of understanding could only be obtained over a considerable period of time spent in observing, in making myself helpful in whatever ways I could, so that I came in time to be accepted and taken for granted as, virtually, a participant in the life of the community.

The hospitality which I enjoyed in Sikh homes was matched by a welcome at the Temple, at the meetings and functions of the Indian Workers' Association and other organizations, and whenever I visited an Indian shop, club, or cinema. For my part, I had to make an effort to learn the Punjabi language, and to acquire a more than superficial understanding of the teachings of the Sikh religion and the history and folklore of the Sikhs.

The climax of this enjoyable task came in 1970, when the generosity of the Winston Churchill Memorial Trust in granting me a Churchill Travelling Fellowship enabled me to spend a total of sixteen weeks in India. I spent thirteen of these weeks in the

[1] Quotations from the *Guru Granth* and, as in this case, the *Dasm Granth* are, unless otherwise stated, from *Sacred Writings of the Sikhs*. Bibliography, section 3.

Punjab, staying for most of the time in villages there, with the relations of some of my Sikh friends in Huddersfield. I managed to see all the districts from which Sikhs have come to live in Huddersfield, and spent long enough in these districts at least to confirm or disprove some of the assumptions that I, and others working with these immigrants, had been making. Once again, the success of the project was due to a large extent to the generous and spontaneous hospitality of the people with whom I stayed. Wherever I stayed a week or two, I was accepted very much as a member of the family. No efforts were spared to help me but life went on in very much the usual way. I was able to watch the daily routine, the work of men and women, to see the games of the children, to take part in religious festivals and local holidays, and to obtain some feeling for the workings of the extended family and the village community, for the ideas of parents on the upbringing of their children, and for the role of religion in their lives.

On the strength of my experience, I could, presumably, have made some contribution to the already fairly substantial literature on the 'background' of immigrants. I felt, however, that such 'background', by itself, is less and less relevant to the actual situation of the children of the immigrant community, Sikh children who have spent the greater part of their lives in Britain, and increasing numbers who have been born here. It seems to me that there is a greater need for an attempt to judge how far the social traditions of the Punjabi villages are being maintained in Sikh households in Britain; or to answer the question, how much use to the teacher, administrator, or social worker is knowledge of the 'background' of these children and their families? To give an account, in effect, not only of what I learnt in India, but of the way in which that experience has illuminated six years' work and friendship with these children and their families.

My essay inevitably reflects a very personal interpretation, and should be read as such; it is a labour of love, and cannot claim to be a dispassionate, systematically researched, or authoritative description. My own interests and enthusiasms are part of it—in superficial ways, such as my experiments with Punjabi cookery, or my preference for Punjabi folk-music rather than the products of the Hindi cinema—but also in my own interpretation of basic attitudes and beliefs of the Sikhs, on religious matters like the nature of the Absolute, the meaning of *Nam*, the function of the *Guru Granth Saheb*, and on social and moral matters like the idea of the family, the privileges and duties of its members, the relationships between parents and children. These are very delicate and complex matters, and are part of the personality of each Sikh child with whom I have come in contact. For anyone, especially an 'outsider' and a non-specialist, to try to understand these things and to try to judge how they affect the personality and behaviour of individual children, requires a degree of arrogance. Seeing how people in a particular community with strong traditions of its own respond to the pressures of life in a complex, pluralistic society can profoundly affect one's own ways of thinking on a much wider range of issues.

But my only justification for what may seem a clumsy invasion of a community's privacy is concern for the children. A teacher can, I believe, through sheer lack of understanding and sympathetic imagination, inflict great harm on a child's feelings and the development of his personality. Yet in my experience a teacher who has a little understanding can sometimes help a child to come to terms with conflicts and anxieties and can discover the special, valuable traits which the combination of Sikh upbringing and his own individuality fosters in him. I hope, therefore, that this personal account will be helpful to teachers who have children of Sikh immigrants in their classes, and to others who work, in professional, administrative, or voluntary capacities for the welfare of these children. We teachers do need to reconsider both what we teach and the way we teach, to re-examine our own attitudes and preconceptions when we deal with multi-racial classes. Teachers of the future, in Colleges and Departments of Education, must regard such rethinking as a necessary part of their preparation to become teachers in modern Britain.

The academic, specialist reader may find much to disagree with, much that I must have oversimplified or approached in a naïve, unscientific way; to him I apologize, in the hope that he will at least find some ideas worth consideration, or some aspects of the situation which I, as one concerned with the immediate practicalities of the classroom, feel could be illuminated by further, more systematic research. The reader who is himself a Sikh may well find he is amused or infuriated by my mistakes, my superficial judgements, or by what I have left unsaid. I am especially conscious that I have not even begun to convey the effect of living in an atmosphere of pervasive hostility and ever-present racialist attitudes. This can only be done honestly and effectively by someone who has experienced it. The criticism of such readers will be especially welcome; the experience of the 'second generation' growing up in Britain is not an easy or a pleasant one, but I am sure it will produce—besides the frustration, bitterness, and despair—some really creative and understanding minds who will be able to put into powerful words what I and other writers can at present only describe in a second-hand way.

My thanks are due to Huddersfield Education Department, and especially to Mr. Trevor Burgin, Educational Organizer for Remedial and Immigrant Education, for all kinds of help and encouragement; to the Chairman, Council, and Director-General of the Winston Churchill Memorial Trust for making possible my visit to the Punjab; and above all to the Sikh community in Huddersfield and to those many families in the Punjab who gave me help and hospitality while I was there. To name individuals would be invidious (and in some cases embarrassing—I hope I have avoided, by guarded treatment of quotations and references, such embarrassment to any person); I have a debt of gratitude to virtually every Sikh family in Huddersfield for some act of hospitality, help, or friendliness. I hope that my efforts to help their children, and to help others to understand their children, will in some measure repay that debt.

Sat Sri Akal.

2 The Punjab and Migration

How did the Sikh families come to be here? Why did they leave their homes in India? Their motive was not grinding poverty—the Sikh state of the Punjab in North-Western India is the most prosperous and rapidly developing part of modern India. It is a very fertile area when adequately watered; as one approaches by train or air, one can see patches of green separated by tracts of sandy brown wasteland; the green patches get bigger as one heads to the north-west, until they join together in a wide green plain with very few pieces of wasteland intervening.

There are three areas within the Punjab State. To the south of the River Sutlej lies Malwa; the largest town in this area is Ludhiana. To the east of Ludhiana is the modern state capital (for the time being shared with Haryana State), Chandigarh; to the west is Ferozepur, and to the south the former princely states of Patiala, Nabha, and Jind. Malwai Sikhs have certain cultural differences from those beyond the Sutlej, but these are not significant for our purposes. Malwai people, especially from Ludhiana District and the adjacent parts of Ferozepur District, have emigrated to many parts of the world; the largest Malwai communities are in Singapore and Malaysia. There are a few Malwais in Huddersfield including members of a family who formerly lived in Singapore, though they still have 'family homes' in the Punjab. They are from the neighbourhood of Ludhiana, and the area to the west of Ludhiana, towards Moga.

North of the Sutlej and east of the Beas River lies the Doab ('two rivers'); the main town here is Jullunder, and Hoshiarpur and Kapurthala are also important. It is from this area that the largest number of Sikhs have come to Britain—there can hardly be a village without some of its people in Britain. The great majority of Sikh families in Huddersfield originate from villages to the south of Jullunder, especially the neighbourhoods of Jandiala and Nakodar, two small towns in the area. Nearly all the 'feeder' villages of Huddersfield are within fifteen miles of Nakodar (west, north, and east) and the majority are within seven miles.

Between the Beas and Ravi rivers lies Majha (the Doab is sometimes included in Majha, too) in which lies the holiest place of the

Sikhs, the city of Amritsar. Majha people consider themselves slightly superior to others, perhaps on account of the special character of Amritsar; they think they speak a 'purer' form of Punjabi, and are disinclined to let their sons marry Malwai or Doabai girls. There are few people from Majha in Huddersfield; those who have come from this region have family connections with Doabais who came here first—for example, a Majhai woman whose husband is a Doabai.

The majority of Sikhs who have come to Huddersfield belong to landowning families. There appear to be two classes of landowners in the Punjab—the 'rural plutocracy', with holdings of 30 acres or more, who own most of the land, and poorer smallholders with 10 acres or less who are more numerous but own less land altogether —there seem to be relatively few landowners between these two categories. These acreages may seem small by British standards, but, in fact, families of eight or more persons are supported quite comfortably by 30 acres of fertile land there. The families of the migrants are very largely in the '30 acre' class, and these are the politically and economically dominant group in the Punjab.

These landowners are known as *Jats*; the *Jats* were historically a group of tribes, many of whom became Sikhs (but there are Hindu and Muslim *Jats*). Historical developments have led to their being regarded as a landowning 'caste', though strictly they have a variety of caste origins (mainly *Vaisya*—the Hindu 'third caste') which have become obscured. Caste exclusiveness was condemned by the Sikh Gurus, and considerable progress has been made in the Punjab towards removing the ill effects of the system, but in the sense that certain groups are regarded as having traditional jobs and marriage-links, it still very much exists.

Besides *Jats*, there are many other 'tribal' groups amongst the Sikhs, most of which overlap with Hindu and Muslim categories. In Huddersfield, there are a few *Ramgarhias* and *Khatris*. The *Ramgarhias* are thought of mainly as *mystris*—craftsmen and mechanics, but many are now prosperous factory-owners in the towns, and they formed the largest group amongst Sikh migrants to East Africa. The *Khatris* are mainly a merchant caste. Elsewhere in Britain there are groups of *Bhatra* Sikhs, traditionally pedlars, but I know of none in Huddersfield. These groupings have been an important factor in Sikh politics—in many towns in Britain the *Ramgarhias* have established separate *Gurdwaras* (Temples), but in Huddersfield there are too few to form a major faction, and the non-*Jats* have generally acted as a neutral, balancing element between rival *Jat* groups.

Sikhs also identify themselves with hereditary *goth* (Hindi *gotra*); this is sometimes called 'sub-caste', but this is not a helpful term— 'clan' might be more appropriate. Generally the majority of people in a village (or district of a large village) belong to the same *goth*, and many village-names derive from *goth*-names. The 'surname' used by many Sikhs—Sidhu, Gill, Bassi, Dhillon and so on—indicates their *goth*.[1]

To the Sikh landowner, his family's holding is the symbol of security, but it has in the past proved unreliable, and, like many peasants, his attitude to the land is ambivalent—the Sikhs are eloquent in singing the praises of their homeland, yet there are over a million Sikhs living in other parts of India, and probably more than that number in other countries. There are many villages in Jullunder Doab where as much as two-thirds of the people whose family home is there, are living abroad (this is apparently true of Jandiala, Shanker, and possibly Nakodar, all quite substantial places to the south of Jullunder).

The tradition of migration has grown up over the last hundred years. Several reasons might be suggested: the most plausible is the pressure of population on the limited amount of fertile land available. When the head of a family dies, his sons may divide up the land amongst themselves—if this means splitting up the holding into uneconomical units, one or more of the younger brothers may be asked to leave home, the other brothers subscribing to his travelling costs and the cost of setting himself up in a new home, and possibly a business.

Experience has taught that money can be made in a city job or abroad, which, if invested in the family farm, can be used for improving the living standard of the family, raising the productivity of the farm, getting children educated, or finding good husbands for sisters and daughters. It is important to realize that the Sikh migrant who works in Britain or elsewhere overseas and continues to send money to support his family is maintaining the essential communal structure of the joint family, just as much as if he remains at home, working on the family's farm. The ambitiousness of the Sikhs, and the desire for 'qualifications' and 'status', have also made them determined to travel, with generally rather vague ideas of undertaking some study or getting the sort of jobs they feel they deserve.

One might also add that the atmosphere of the extended family

---

[1] It is well-known that Sikh personal names are followed by Singh or Kaur, titles applied by Guru Gobind Singh apparently in an attempt to erase caste-distinction amongst his followers. However, the *goth*-name is widely used as a 'surname' amongst men; some *goths* are purely *Jat*, others overlap several caste-groups. The village-name, trade-name, or even a nickname may be used in the same way—this occurs in Britain when, in casual conversation, 'Gian Singh Lockwood' is distinguished from 'Gian Singh Fartown' or 'Surjit Singh Conductor' from 'Surjit Singh Weaver'. It would obviously make life easier for administrators if all Sikhs were to use a family surname, but there are many who feel that this is strictly contrary to the Guru's wishes and socially divisive. Women seldom use *goth* names, but they may adopt their husband's in imitation of British custom, e.g., Mrs. Hardip Kaur Grewal—otherwise she is just Mrs. (Sardarni) Hardip Kaur ('Mrs. Singh' is wrong but does occur); girls do not normally use their father's *goth* names, except, again, in imitation of British custom.

and the village community can prove stifling to young people, and there may just be a wish to 'break free', perhaps precipitated by some family or village quarrel. For example, a man whose wife quarrels with his mother may find domestic peace by leaving the joint family and setting up a new household in Britain. Similarly, a joint family may be broken up by quarrels between the wives of two brothers—say, over the interests of their respective children and the amount of the family's wealth being expended on the education or marriage of different children. Again, there may be jealousy between brothers if they feel that father is treating one more favourably than another in some way. Many Sikhs would say that the reason they left home was some quarrel of this kind, but it is significant that they accept the joint family as the 'ideal' situation, and explain their decision to leave it in terms of a failure of other members of the family to adhere to the 'rules' of mutual obligation.

For many village people, the opportunities offered by the nearest large town were sufficient, and there has been a continuous movement of people from the villages into the metropolitan centres over the last hundred years—for the Sikhs this has generally meant Delhi. Of course, the urge to move has not been consistently strong —when things have been going well for farmers, the desire to leave the land has died down.

There has also been migration to other rural areas. In the 1880s, the Canal Colonies in the West Punjab were formed, and large numbers of villages in the Lyallpur, Montgomery, and Gujrat areas were colonized by Sikhs. This brought a wave of prosperity which proved illusory; by the end of the century, much of the land in the Punjab was mortgaged to money-lenders, and the urge to find a better living was again strong. The movement to towns continued, and cheap virgin land in the United Provinces was settled and cultivated.

The Partition of 1947 caused the largest movement of population in Sikh history; the large Sikh colonies in West Punjab (Canal Colonies and Lahore) and settlements in the towns of Sindh and North West Frontier Province were abandoned; the refugees were settled in abandoned properties in East Punjab, but there was not enough for all of them; others had to cultivate waste land in South Punjab and North Rajasthan (Sri Ganganagar) and in other parts of India.

The social and psychological effect of this experience on the entire Sikh population, even those who stayed where they were in East Punjab, must have been drastic. The adult Sikhs who migrated to Britain in the 1960s were children or young men at this time; some were refugees themselves, and all of them witnessed the flight of terror-stricken refugees and the killings committed on both sides. Partition affected every family in one way or another. Some have memories of sheltering Muslims in their own homes from Sikh fanatics, or of catering for numbers of long-forgotten relatives from the West Punjab who arrived as refugees, or of the upheaval in their villages when the Muslim weavers and craftsmen left and no one knew how to ply these trades.

So the Sikhs do not belong to villages where life has gone on unchanged for hundreds of years; historical upheavals, bursts of economic expansion (as at the present time), and sudden setbacks in prosperity have contributed to an unsettled tradition.

The first Sikhs who went overseas were troops serving in the army of British India; after 1857, Sikhs played a major role in this army. From the 1880s onwards, they were posted to stations in South East Asia and the Far East. Enterprising men saw opportunities in these places for setting up various businesses and returned as civilians, forming the nuclei of Sikh colonies that still survive in some cities in these areas, notably Singapore. They soon extended their activities to Thailand, the Philippines, and Fiji. In the early 1900s, they began to travel in the wake of Chinese migrants from Hong Kong, to British Columbia, where they worked as labourers on the Canadian Pacific Railway, and later settled as farm labourers, farmers, and lumberjacks. From Canada, there was a movement south into Washington, Oregon, and California. It was in Canada and the U.S.A. that Sikh migrants first encountered white racialism. Life was made exceedingly unpleasant for them, and many returned to India between 1910 and 1915, but some had settled and started farms or businesses—they weathered the storm and their communities are still flourishing, joined by many more migrants in the 1950s and more recently.

During the first part of the present century, other important Sikh settlements were established in East and South Africa, mainly by merchants of the *Ramgarhia* caste (though at first they went as labourers on the railways), and the Persian Gulf. Students and a few businessmen were in London and other European capitals by 1914; in the inter-war years, the Indian door-to-door salesmen began to appear in Britain. A Sikh engaged in this sort of trade bought a house in Huddersfield in the 1930s (his grandson is there now, but the family left during the war, so there is not a continuous history of settlement). There are one or two Sikhs in Huddersfield now who were elsewhere in Britain before 1939, for example, a family who were living in Glasgow before that date.

The first Sikhs to arrive in Huddersfield after the war came via Bradford. They had acquired some abandoned land in 1947, and, on the strength of this, two cousins came to Bradford in 1952 and 1956 respectively; they were engaged in house-to-house selling of nylon stockings and such things. By 1958, they had moved to Huddersfield and lodged with some Gujeratis, who had come from Walsall and bought a house in the Folly Hall area (at that time a district of small terraced houses immediately adjacent to the mills and factories along the canal, to the south of the town centre). Most of the Gujeratis moved elsewhere, but the Sikhs stayed and were joined by other members of the family. They bought two adjacent shops in Spring Grove, an area of more substantial terraced houses to the west of the town centre, built as good-class Victorian family homes, but more recently occupied by poorer working people and by immigrants from Ireland and East Europe.

One of the cousins returned to India, but the other men stayed; they began to buy houses which they rented to incoming Sikh immigrants, many of whom were related to the original two or were connected with them in some way.

The first Sikhs to migrate from the Punjab to Britain were mostly young men, many of them still unmarried. They came to join the 'pioneer' settlers, to whom they were generally related or with whom they had some contacts. Many arrived at London Airport with a list of 'contacts'—relations, fellow-villagers, friends, school-fellows, and more remote connections—with whom they would stay while seeking work. They often started in Southall, where the biggest Sikh settlement in Britain was forming; if they could not find work there, they moved on to places where opportunities were rumoured to exist. In the late fifties there was a chronic shortage of unskilled and semi-skilled labour which affected Huddersfield's textile industry quite severely, so there were plenty of jobs available —in service industries and public transport as well as in the textile mills. Housing was cheap and relatively plentiful; new arrivals lived in houses near the town centre owned, very often, by a relation or friend who charged a minimal rent for lodgings. Conditions were not good, with houses turned into dormitories, the men cooking for themselves and neglecting their own welfare to a large extent.

The ambitions of these men were rather vague: some had ideas of making money with a view to an early return to their homeland, where they would use the capital to set up some business; others had hopes of obtaining skills and qualifications that would stand them in good stead if they returned; others realized that they would have to stay abroad for a long time, possibly all their working lives, if they were to achieve and maintain the standard of living they desired for themselves and their dependants. At first, the inflow reflected fairly closely the demand for labour in the area, with immigrants coming and going as job opportunities became available; the 'panic' that preceded the enforcement of the first Immigration Act seems to have disturbed this—a lot of men who were not sure whether to come or not were forced to make up their minds before it was 'too late'.

So, in the period of 1958-62, a substantial number of young Sikh men came to settle in the area to the west of the town centre.

The 1962 census recorded 501 Indians in the town.[1] The majority of them had little knowledge of English, and no experience of work in large-scale industries. Jobs were obtained mainly through hearsay, via the network of family and village contacts spread through several towns up and down the country. As a result, a single enterprising Indian in a mill or foundry could act as an 'agent' for his employer, finding men amongst his own family-village group to fill vacancies for unskilled workers; this led to the formation of all-Indian 'work-gangs' on some shifts, with the English-speaking 'job-fixer' interpreting the management's instructions to the whole group.

Most of the men found heavy, dirty, or repetitive jobs, the jobs least favoured by other workers. They were willing to work long hours, on night and weekend shifts. Employers, in effect, used them as a 'last resort', but found satisfactory workers, hard-working and willing to stick at these jobs.

They were very vulnerable to exploitation: Indian landlords and 'job-fixers' were in a position to extract a lot of money from them, though the ethics of the village-family system made those who did this social outcasts in the end. There were cases of 'white' foremen collaborating with 'job-fixers' in rackets, extracting money from Indian workers in exchange for jobs. The 'work-gangs' were isolated from the other workers, and there was little possibility of drawing them into trade union organization, so there was a serious danger of wage-rates being undermined; this fear, mixed with distrust of strangers, led to ill feeling amongst white workers.

Working long hours and living very cheaply, they accumulated plenty of money, which they used to pay off the cost of coming to Britain (this was generally contributed by the joint family, as a kind of 'investment' in the member who migrated—the returns on the investment were generally very substantial) and sent home to help their families. The money was generally sent in monthly instalments, either by money-order, or by arrangement with illegal money-changers who (in order to obtain much-needed foreign exchange with which to buy gold to smuggle into India) would arrange the delivery of rupees to the migrant's family up to 50% more than the official exchange value of the sterling paid to him.

Evidence of the difference this money made to the life of the Punjabi villagers is clearly visible today. The families of the migrants have *pakka* brick-built houses, with electric lighting and fans. Their farms are watered by electric pumps ('tube wells'); many have tractors (though import restrictions make these difficult to obtain, since 1968 it has been possible for Indians in England to send tractors to their relatives), trailers, seed-drills, threshing

[1] I am indebted to John Goodall's article in the Institute of Race Relations' *Newsletter* (October 1966), Bibliography, section 10, for statistical information in this chapter.

machines, and other farm machinery. Some have used the capital to set up small industrial enterprises in the towns (usually related to agriculture, such as servicing agricultural machinery) to supplement the income from their farms, to invest in more farmland or livestock, or to buy lorries to set up a haulage business.

In effect, while migration represented a 'break' from the physical closeness of the joint family, the economic structure of the family was, to a considerable extent, maintained. Instead of farming land in common, members of a family where some men had migrated became partners in an extended enterprise with individuals contributing in a variety of different ways to the benefit of all. Their money has raised family standards of living; girls can obtain more educated or wealthy husbands, the old and sick can get medical care, servants and farm labourers can be hired, and children can be educated at secondary schools and colleges. In many villages, community projects have been undertaken using money contributed by people in Britain and the voluntary co-operative labour of the villagers—building or extending schools, constructing *pakka* metalled roads to the village, building health centres, *Dharmsalas* ('village halls'), *Gurdwaras*, and so on. The remarkable economic progress of the Punjab State over the last few years can be ascribed about equally to the building of the Bhakra Dam and related works, providing electricity and water to most of the state, to the development of high-yielding strains of wheat, and to the inflow of earned wealth from migrants in Britain and North America.

In time, a few of the Sikhs in Huddersfield obtained semi-skilled jobs, as spinners, weavers, pattern-makers, even with supervisory roles, but there was little access to skilled jobs, or to jobs not considered 'working class' in status. This was felt most keenly by those who had come with the highest ambitions and expectations, especially those who had had a full education in India (at least up to 'matriculation', school-leaving standard). The movement of 'white' workers away from unskilled jobs had not extended to skilled trades and crafts; such trades are highly unionized, and very strict rules define apprenticeship and entry to them. Lack of English made office or shop work impossible, though even those whose English was quite fluent encountered discrimination in seeking 'white collar' jobs. Supervisory jobs were only available where the Indian would be in charge of an all-immigrant 'work-gang'. The best they could hope for was jobs that were 'clean', relatively light, yet still offering plenty of overtime or piecework; there was a chronic shortage of labour on the corporation buses, and a very substantial number of English-speaking Sikhs began to work as conductors and subsequently as drivers.

So the community of men around the 'pioneers' grew rapidly, and a hierarchy began to develop, the leaders being the 'pioneers'—landlords, 'job-fixers', shopkeepers, and others on whom the majority had to depend for some reason (anyone who could speak, read, or write English was in great demand as an agent for any dealings with officialdom, and so they acquired standing in the community) —and the articulate, ambitious, and frustrated 'élite' centred on the public transport service.

As time went on, the migrants who were already married asked their wives and children to join them, and the younger men brought girls (selected, of course, by their parents) to marry them. With the advent of wives and children, the character of the community changed. Instead of living very frugally in all-male households they set up family homes. The habit of working long hours, especially nights and weekends, in order to raise maximum wages, was gradually abandoned. Instead of sending the greater part of their earnings to their family in India in regular instalments, the men began to spend it in Britain on consumer goods for their families, and domestic luxuries like cars and televisions. As more and more 'single family' households were set up, with the man as owner-occupier, a lot of social problems were alleviated—overcrowding, health hazards, rack-renting, prostitution, and homosexuality.

But the tendency was not in all respects towards adoption of 'British' ways of life. Shops selling Indian food and clothes were opened in the areas where the families settled—the areas of smaller but generally rather superior terraced houses to the south and east of the town (Thornton Lodge and Fartown especially).[1] A *Gurdwara* was established, holding *Sangats* (assemblies) at first in the Labour Party's Meeting Rooms, and later acquiring and converting a big house in Bath Street, near to the Spring Grove and Fartown settlements and to the town centre. Political organization developed, of which the Indian Workers' Association is the most important, organized by left-wingers mostly working on the buses. Clubs were formed to show Indian films, and the Empire Cinema has been hired on Sunday mornings and afternoons for this purpose for several years.

The effect of this growth of a community, with Sikhs catering for the needs of their own people in many different ways, was that the sense of being Sikhs was strengthened, and adherence to the customs of the community—in such matters as marriage arrangements and religious observances—became more important than it had been. Links with the extended family 'back home' are maintained through letters sent two or three times a year, and money is still sent very generously, if less regularly, in times of emergency, or to meet occasional family expenditure, as at the weddings of sisters.

By 1964, there were about 540 Sikhs in Huddersfield, of whom nearly one-third were children under 14; another third were aged

---

[1] There was a lot of demolition in the part of Spring Grove nearest the town centre, 1964-5 (building of Civic Centre) and 1971 (building of ring road).

15-29, and about a quarter of these were women; nearly all the rest were under 49, and there were relatively more older women, 'indicating the high proportion of stabilized families amongst the Sikhs'.[1] Some Indian children had been admitted at Spring Grove County School as early as 1958, and by 1961 there were 116 children there from Commonwealth countries, the majority of whom were Sikhs. Large numbers came up to 1965, after which they were outnumbered by Pakistanis—Pakistani men (from areas in the West Punjab) had begun to settle in the town soon after the Indians; they were less quick to bring their wives and children to join them, but by 1964 they substantially outnumbered the Sikhs—and by West Indians, mainly from Jamaica and the Windward Islands. The Pakistani and West Indian immigrants settled in the same parts of the town initially, many of the West Indians lodging in houses owned by Indians and using some of the services provided by Indians—notably the food-shops and the social clubs. Enterprising Indian shopkeepers began to stock sweet potatoes, salt fish, and other Caribbean foods; many items in the Indian diet—aubergines, okra, and so on—are liked by West Indians too.

By now, the immigrant men were reconsidering their plans; it became clear to them that they would have to stay for a long time, possibly all their working lives. They could see little hope of returning to India with enough money to keep them comfortably there, the demands of the extended family for financial help continued to be insistent, the Immigration Act had made it difficult to come and go at will. They were still unwilling to commit themselves, but they became increasingly reconciled to staying 'unless we're thrown out'. Their hopes for jobs or training giving status were largely dashed, but they were able to make enough money to help their families in India, and to maintain their wives, children, and sometimes elderly dependants in Britain. They were able to enjoy the company of other Sikhs, their tastes in food, clothes, and entertainment were catered for, as well as their communal interests—religion and politics. The *gora* ('white') community may be mysterious, stand-offish, or even openly hostile, but there was no need to have much to do with it at any but the most formal, official level.

By the late 1960s, the Sikh community in Huddersfield could be said to be fully established. There were few married men whose wives had not joined them, so the number of new arrivals dropped to a trickle—a few elderly dependants, a number of families who had lived elsewhere in Britain, and some who had been back to India for an extended 'holiday'. By 1969 they numbered about 1,300, the great majority being under 40—adults of child-bearing age, and children growing up—a generation of 'British Sikhs'.

[1] Goodall, op. cit.

3   Family, Infancy, and Childhood

The most important element in the Sikh community anywhere in the world is the family. The individual man, woman, or child sees himself, and is seen by others, firstly as a part of a family; it is impossible to have much understanding of the individual Sikh child without knowing something of his family.

'Family' means, of course, the extended family, which is the main social unit in the Punjab; even there, a fair number of extended families have split up in recent years, with younger sons leaving the family home during the lifetime of the head of the family, but it is probably fair to say that two-thirds of the *Jat* Sikhs in villages are living in classic extended-family households. Moreover, people who have left the family home, even those who have gone overseas, are very much conscious of the bonds of duty and affection within the family, and these continue to influence their behaviour in many ways.[1]

The extended family is 'based' at the home of the senior male member; the distinction between 'house' and 'home' is a difficult one for anyone learning English as a second language—for the British Sikh there is the added complication that 'home' is, in a very real sense, the family home in the Punjab. For the Sikh child born in England, on the other hand, it is his own father's house, here, and the Punjab is imagined—even the children who were born in India and came to England at seven or ten years old remember that 'home' in a vague way, with the very nice and very nasty aspects heightened in their memory. They may remember freedom they had in the fields, the delicious sweetness of mangoes in the summer, the nearness of doting grandparents, uncles and aunts; but others only remember the scorching heat, the snakes and creeping things, or the depressing schools.

When the head of a family dies, his eldest son succeeds to the *pagri* (a new turban wound on his head as a token of his authority when the period of mourning for his father has ended, and his ashes have been scattered at a holy river or bathing-place), although his

[1] I am grateful to Dr. Roger Ballard of the Ethnic Relations Research Unit, Bristol University, for letting me see his unpublished paper, 'Family Organisation Among the Sikhs in England', and for the opportunity for us to 'compare notes'.

widow retains a good deal of respect and ultimate authority in certain matters—marriage arrangements, disputes over the family property, and so on. The family property is normally divided equally amongst the sons; the eldest son is responsible for the education and marriage arrangements of his brothers and sisters who are minors.[1] Often, the head of a family in the Punjab will farm land jointly with his brothers, but it is as likely that they will leave the family home at the time the land is divided and establish a new household.

For the *Jat* Sikh, the land-holding is his main capital and security; he will only sell it if he is very hard up, or doing very well in a city job or overseas. If he decides to sell, he is subject to the will of the head of the family, and can be legally blocked by any member of the family who has any claim on the property, for himself or his heirs (so that a man with no male children might be prevented from selling his land by a younger brother whose sons should inherit it). Thus, for the first generation at least, 'home' is the family 'base' in the Punjab. Houses occupied in Britain, or elsewhere in India, by junior members of the family, may be bought and sold but it is very rarely that the 'family home' is sold. The relative readiness of Britons to sell their houses and remove their entire household surprises Indians—their own mobility is different, because they always have the sense of a fixed original 'home' at the back of their minds. For their children, if they never visit there, or only briefly, this may be too vague.

This short account of the organization of the extended family in its classic setting might help to make clear the way in which, even at 'long range', it can establish a degree of economic, social, and emotional equilibrium; on the other hand, it is by no means proof against internal tensions: the system I have described can obviously produce dissension over the property, and the same applies to the emotional patterns of affection and duty within the family. The family may provide a stable and secure environment in which everyone has a clearly defined, and valued, role, but personal distress and quarrels can, and regularly do, develop as a result of conflicting loyalties and aspirations.

This is the background to the family life of the Sikhs in Britain. Migration has imposed severe strains on the system; the type of housing available in this country is only suitable for families of four or five, so when brothers, and other groups of male relatives, living together in 'all-male households' were joined by their wives and children, they had to establish new, single-family households,

---

[1] A man is also responsible for the widow and orphans of a deceased brother. He may 'marry' his widowed sister-in-law by the simple ceremony of 'taking her under his *chaddar* (mantle)'; this is often only a technicality, but it is recognized as a legal form of marriage in the Punjab, and is the only case in which a Sikh may be said to practise polygamy—it is nearly always the explanation for the occasional cases of a Sikh husband with more than one wife in Britain.

with husband, wife, children, and possibly one or two male relatives as lodgers, waiting for their own wives to come. Older relatives sometimes come to join their sons and grandchildren, but this is rare—it means abandoning the family home, and the change in climate and way of life is not welcome to older people.

But the sense of belonging to a larger group is very much there—in the 'best room' (that is, the room reserved mainly for entertaining guests, usually the 'front room' of a larger terraced or semi-detached house) of a Sikh home in England, there will be a gallery of family photos, including, very often, photos of deceased heads of the family taken at their laying-out. Whether a Sikh is at his family home or 5,000 miles away, his links with the family are almost a part of his nervous system; families are reunited at weddings, and in times of sickness or bereavement, and the family (rather than, say, the state or the *Gurdwara*) is the body to which the individual looks for financial and practical help, as well as emotional support in any crisis. Links with the family in India are maintained by letter-writing, not necessarily very frequent but at least two or three times a year; often, as we have mentioned, the Sikhs in Britain are sending money regularly, and they certainly give financial help to members of the family in India whenever it is needed for some special purpose. The desire to go back for a visit is always quite strong, and is fed by requests from people there when a man has been away for many years. It is a kind of permanent 'good intention', but amongst the first generation there is often the uncertainty about how long they will stay in Britain—a decision to visit India for a holiday is an admission that they will be staying in Britain at least till the children grow up. It is expensive to take one's family by air; the possibility, open to Pakistanis, of going by road is virtually removed as Indians cannot drive through Pakistan. Thus, most men have been 'home' or are seriously planning to do so; some of them plan to take their wives—or for their wives to go alone to visit their families; few have taken their children yet, but it is likely that more will in the future. Whether they actually see India or not—the family 'home', the relations whose photos decorate the living-room, the *Durbar Saheb* at Amritsar—will surely be a factor influencing the children's attitude to the beliefs and traditions of their parents.

The extended-family system also functions within Britain. We have mentioned how members of a family would help each other in the early days of migration, providing lodging and information about jobs. There is much travelling about the country, visiting relatives in different towns; the western 'summer holiday' is not yet popular amongst the immigrants—the problems of finding suitable accommodation for a 'seaside holiday' prove a deterrent —so Sikh children are likely to spend their holidays in Southall or Wolverhampton. As a result, they become aware of circles of adults and children besides their neighbours and school friends, who are important in the circle of relatives, friends and others with whom the child has contact and in whom he is interested. They are often very much attached to cousins who live in another town.

The strength of the family ties provides practical and emotional support to the individual, but it also places his behaviour under the close scrutiny of the rest of the family. Even when a family is spread over the world, news about the doings of each of its members circulates quite quickly—as well as letters and visits amongst members of the family, there is gossip amongst neighbours in the 'home' village in the Punjab, who also have relatives in Britain sending news of their friends. This can lead to great unhappiness. Immigrant parents might to some extent sympathize with the aspiration of their sons and (more particularly) daughters for the 'freedom' enjoyed by western teenagers; they are not entirely tyrannous or reactionary, they have themselves 'broken away' to some extent and are aware of the attractions of a different way of life. But they are subject to pressure from their own elders, and fear for the good name of their family in the Punjab, amongst people who know little about life in western cities. And there is always the fear at the back of the parents' minds, that their daughter's chances of a good marriage will be ruined if there are rumours in the villages near their own that she has succumbed to 'western' behaviour. The sanctions on an individual's behaviour that exist in the extended family household are maintained when the family is split up.

The elderly head of the family retains ultimate authority in the family on all matters of importance, but he is expected to refrain from committing himself on small, day-to-day affairs—he leaves his sons to haggle with merchants over prices, for example. Indian custom expects him to detach himself from worldly concerns, and to concentrate his attention on religious matters; however, many quite aged men insist on working in the fields as energetically as their sons and grandsons—there is probably more piety amongst old ladies, who do sometimes sit all day repeating the Name of God. The old are treated with great respect; their sons, grandchildren and daughters-in-law greet them by touching their feet and embracing their legs. It is not done to disagree with an old person, or to question anything he says, even when he is in his 'second childhood' (indeed, the very young and the very old are treated with the same indulgence). However, one does not feel that these families are, in general, dominated by a petty tyrant—the head of the family knows that his own peace of mind, as well as the happiness of the whole family, depends on his own reasonableness in dealing with his juniors.

The head of the family in India may intervene in the affairs of his children and grandchildren in Britain; he will certainly be concerned about the marriage arrangements of his grandsons and granddaughters, and will try to take an interest in the way in which they are being brought up and educated. However from day to day the British Sikh children will regard as head of their family not an aged patriarch, as they would in the Punjab, but their young father, a man who has to be away from home all day (and in many cases he works in the evening, at nights or weekends), who is harassed with all the routine responsibilities of keeping his immediate family, as well as by the pressures and demands from the rest of his extended family.

In this situation, the other major link in the Punjabi family assumes even greater importance—besides respect for elders, the strongest nexus within the family is between sons or daughters and their mother. A mother is regarded as the anchor of the family —we shall discuss her role in detail as we go on to consider children growing up; suffice to say for the moment, that attachment to mother, and possibly mother-dominance, must be considered a very strong factor in the character of Sikh men, and must be taken into account in considering the respective roles of men and women in the community.

Moreover, the link between mother and daughter is as strong; a consequence of this is rather frequent tension between wife and mother-in-law—the wife longs for her father's home and the sympathy of her own mother, while the husband's loyalties are strained between his wife and his mother; this is a recurrent theme in Punjabi stories, and a subject of many folk-songs both sentimental and humorous. Migration, and the increasing wealth of *Jat* farmers, has made it a realistic proposition for a man whose wife does not get on well with his mother, to leave the joint family and set up a new household in India or abroad.

Reverence for grandfather and mother is, of course, a common feature of many societies, but there is another bond of affection that seems to be peculiarly strong in Punjabi culture—that between brother and sister; this, again, is frequently referred to in folklore— it is symbolized by the ritual of *Tikka*, when girls put saffron on their brothers' foreheads and garlands of marigolds round their necks, and the boys promise to protect their sisters.[1] The classic historical example is Nanaki, Guru Nanak's devoted sister; in legend, the tragedy of *Mirza Sahiban* turns on Sahiban's agonizing choice between the lives of her lover and of her brothers—it is her lover who has to die; this almost fanatical dedication to a brother's welfare is also seen in the historical story of Rani Saheb

[1] This is done a couple of days after *Diwali*, perhaps because Sikh warriors used to return home to their families for this festival, the main Sikh 'time of reunion', and they would promise to remember their sisters and defend their honour before leaving home again. It is obviously similar to the Hindu *Raksh Bandhan*, but the Punjabis do not tie a thread on the boy's wrist, and *Raksh Bandhan* is celebrated in the monsoon season, not at *Diwali*.

Kaur leading an army to defend her brother's lands. This affection, again, can be a source of tension; there are matters, generally of a petty nature—choice of clothes, giving or receiving gifts, entertaining a guest—in which a man may heed the opinion of his sister more than that of his wife.

It follows from this that a special bond of affection exists between a woman and her brother's children; in the joint family home, an unmarried younger sister helps to look after a man's children. Actually, there is a good deal of attachment between all categories of uncles and aunts and their nieces and nephews, which is important in times of crisis—when parents die or fall ill or are separated from the children for any reason.[1]

This simplified description of the extended family, and something of its internal structure, may help teachers and others who deal with Sikh families to understand its complexities. It is not a despotic structure; decisions are made jointly, and the interests of younger members, including the women and children, are voiced and taken into account, even though the head of the family—either the ultimate head at the family home in the Punjab, or the immediate head in Britain—will act as the spokesman and executive in dealing with outsiders. It may show some of the demands that can be made on the individual Sikh by members of his family apart from his own wife and children, and, conversely, the sources of help to which he can turn in difficulty. Most important, it is the framework in which Sikh children are being brought up in Britain, an essential part of their emotional environment which is markedly different from the background of other children, and which must be taken into account by those who want to understand them.

The children of Sikhs in Britain are being brought up in ways which their mothers learnt from their mothers in the Punjab, though these ways are modified to an increasing extent by the differences in the environment—the house, food, health considerations and so on, and, perhaps most important, the absence of the rest of the extended family. Teachers, especially those in Nursery and Infants Schools, who are responsible for increasing numbers of 'local born' Sikh children, need to know something of the life of these children in their formative years, especially the way the parents expect to look after their young children, and the way the parents expect the children to develop.

Societies with strong social and religious traditions, like that of the *Jat* Sikhs, see growing up, and indeed the whole cycle of human life, as a kind of ritual or sacramental progression. The birth of a baby, and landmarks in a child's development are marked

---

[1] It is perhaps significant that the Punjabi language distinguishes five categories of 'uncle': Father's older brother; father's younger brother; father's sister's husband; mother's brother; and mother's sister's husband. There are four categories of 'aunt', and paternal and maternal grandparents are distinguished.

by a great many simple rites—these are not necessarily 'religious' in the western sense of the word, in that they are not (with certain exceptions) prescribed in the teachings of the Sikh Gurus, but, as we shall see, the distinction between 'religious' and 'social' traditions is largely a western invention, irrelevant in discussing this community. The rites associated with various stages in childhood include ritual actions and songs; they reflect a conception of the development and socialization of the child that is handed down from mother to daughter.

The presence of older women in the extended family must be a great help to a Punjabi woman when her children are born, especially during her first confinement, when she may go to her own mother for care and sympathy. This sort of help is not usually available to the Sikh woman in Britain, and doctors, midwives or health visitors cannot replace the emotional support it gives. A few have returned to India soon after the birth of a baby, so as to have the help of their mothers and sisters in caring for it.

In households where a conscious attempt is being made to maintain the Sikh way of life, the round of ritual begins as soon as the baby is born; the first part of the *Japji Saheb* (that is, the first words of the *Guru Granth*) may be whispered in the baby's ear. If the baby is a boy, there are celebrations—in Britain, this usually means inviting friends and relations to a meal and drinks. There are hymns (*Shabads*) in the *Guru Granth Saheb* appropriate to the occasion, such as the hymn of Guru Arjan Dev on the birth of his son:

> The true Lord has sent a Great Soul,
> Blessed is the Child born from His Spirit.
> When the Child came in the womb of his mother
> Great was her joy and ecstasy.
> A son is born, a devoted child of God.
> The child comes from the Lord
> He is born in His Spirit.
> (*Rag Asa*, MV, p. 396, translated by Trilochan Singh in *Guru Tegh Bahadur*.)

and lyrics for folk-song and dance. These songs generally refer to children as 'gifts from God'; for a soul to enter the world in human form is, of course, regarded as a great blessing, won after many thousands of less fortunate incarnations—this point is made in hymns for birth-celebrations, as well as the corollary, the great responsibility that the care and upbringing of children places on the parents. Here the space available for dancing is inadequate, but at a 'birth-party' there is always some uncle or brother ready to sing or recite a poem of congratulations. Parents are expected (as at weddings and other festivities) to entertain as generously as they can afford, and may give gifts to the *Gurdwara* or to some Sikh charity in celebration.

The baby's name is generally chosen by opening the *Guru Granth Saheb* at random and finding the first letter on the page—the child's name has to begin with this letter; this ceremony is generally carried out in Britain at the *Gurdwara*, when the parents first attend a *Sangat* (congregation) after the baby is born, so there may be a lapse of a few weeks before he has an 'official' name. Punjabi names, especially amongst village *Jats* were traditionally quite simple—Joga, Bugga, Buta, Jhumma, Jeet—but there is a fashion now, followed by Sikhs in Britain, for compounds, in which certain affixes feature very commonly—*sur-*, *gur-*, *sat-*, *-jit*, *-nam*, *-inder*, *-dev*, *-pal*, *-dip*. Little attention is paid to the 'meaning' of the name, and most names do for boys or girls (we find Kamaljit Singh, 'water lily-conqueror-lion', Ranjit Kaur, 'battlefield-conquering princess', Harkanwal Singh, 'God's Lotus').[1]

Nicknames are a feature of Punjabi life; babies are always given a simple, often reduplicated name, that must be a help in learning to talk—'Guggi' is less of a mouthful than 'Harbhagwan'. These nicknames may be abbreviations of the personal name—Baksho, Jitu, Raju, Biro—or purely fanciful—Kaka (baby boy), Guddi (baby girl), Pinko, Mina, Titu, Babli;[2] some English names have been adopted to this purpose—Tony, Ricky, Sheila, Lovely. These names are used within the family throughout childhood. Indeed, the less 'babyish' names may stick to a person all through his life, so that he will hardly use his personal name at all, and may have difficulty in remembering it for official purposes in form-conscious Britain—and it must cause no surprise that a child entering Infants School may not know his 'own' name, nor answer to it.

Other landmarks in a child's early life include weaning (sometimes quite late, even in the child's second year, and feeding bottles are used by some mothers for two or three year olds), learning to crawl and to talk, and the first time his or her hair is plaited. There are traditional songs or little rituals for mother and sisters to perform at all these times, though these customs are not observed universally even in the Punjab, and the detail may vary from place to place, even from family to family. Toilet-training is, of course, another important step, though I don't know of any songs on the subject! In India it seems to be left relatively late, and little pressure is put on the young child to exercise control, but the indoor life in Britain makes earlier conformity to accepted standards desirable, and Sikh parents seem to have adopted the methods advocated by health visitors, etc.

The young child is always close to mother. He probably sleeps beside her at night (little attempt is made, incidentally, to control

---

[1] Sikhs change their personal names sometimes when they are adults; it is not uncommon for a bride to be given a new name by her in-laws.

[2] The ending of -o or -u is a familiar or affectionate form, thus 'Ranu' from 'Rani', 'Bapu' from 'Bap', etc.

the time when a young child sleeps or wakes); whenever he cries she breast-feeds him or soothes him with a lullaby;[1] dummies are used to the second or third year. It is mother who elicits the first 'baby talk', which is very much encouraged, with its characteristic reduplication of simplified syllables and consonant substitution: *toti* for *roti* and so on.

Thus the child's first, and overwhelmingly dominant relationship is this absolute mutual dependence between mother and child; mutual, because there is no doubt that a Punjabi girl is brought up to find her fulfilment in caring for her young children. This closeness to mother is a feature of Punjabi family life, but it is strengthened in the British situation. Here, apart from older sisters, there are no other female relatives to substitute for mother at times—probably no grandmother or aunts to help with looking after baby, playing and talking with him—and father too is away all day, so the baby spends most of his time in the solitary company of mother. Even quite big children turn to their mothers for the sort of demonstrative love and sympathy that is taken for granted in the family home with its sense of physical 'closeness'.

On the other hand, there is a good deal of encouragement to independent-mindedness; once a little child can walk and talk, he is free to wander around the home, expecting and receiving kind attentions, finding adults and older brothers and sisters ready to play with him, and few restrictions on his behaviour. The family play with him and talk to him; all this attention must be of enormous value in enabling the child to interpret the social and natural world around him, laying the foundations of his social behaviour and learning ability in later childhood.

The young Sikh child's experience of the world outside his home is not as limited as that of some English children or children of other immigrant communities; Sikh mothers go shopping at the Indian shops, and in the supermarkets and bigger shops in town where their lack of English will not embarrass them; the weekly open market is also a popular shopping place, and baby is taken on shopping expeditions. There will be outings to the park or playground, and baby is taken to the *Gurdwara* with the rest of the family—or even to the Indian film shows. As we have seen, visits to relatives elsewhere in Britain replace conventional 'holidays', but even these present the young child with a wealth of new experiences. The Sikh child is less likely than a child of middle-class British parents to be taken to the seaside or the zoo,

---

[1] *Lori*—an important and attractive genre in Punjabi folk-music; typical lyrics promise sweets—*ladu*—to a 'good baby', or ask sleep to come quickly to 'visit' the child (sleep replies 'I have to visit three or four children then I shall come quickly to your baby') or say that Daddy will drive away any nasty creatures; children of seven or eight years old have told me that they like their mothers to sing a *Lori* before they sleep.

but more and more car-owning Sikh parents are finding their way to these places.

Little children are expected and encouraged to inquire, explore and ask questions; they learn to speak to adults politely but confidently—there is no question of their being 'seen and not heard', and so they learn the valuable skills of making clear what they want, explaining themselves and seeking information; at the same time, their ability to interpret language and situations, and to solve problems, is developed. On the other hand, the social and ethical framework in which their awareness develops is, in a technical sense, 'restricted': experiment and questioning enable the child to acquire practical skills, but the requirements of the social environment, that is, the sort of behaviour expected of each person within the family hierarchy, is taken for granted, and is not a subject for 'discussion'; similarly, religious beliefs and assumptions about right or wrong behaviour in the wider social sphere are learnt, not from explanations, but by the example of the rest of the family in daily life. The rituals marking stages in a child's life, like those marking the turning of the year, seem to assert this unquestioning acceptance of one's *Dharam* or duty— the world is a 'region of duty' and everything in it is fulfilling its *Dharam*; man's *Dharam* is to live in society, and everything he does is a significant part of this duty; thus, eating a healthy diet, keeping clean, observing conventions of dress and so on, are important—probably more important than subscribing to a set of beliefs of a metaphysical kind that we would call 'religion'. The implications of this should become clearer when we discuss other aspects of upbringing and parents' attitudes.

There is clearly much that is valuable in the way Sikh parents raise their young children; it is, of course, a traditional pattern developed in a rural environment and a warm climate, and some adjustment is needed to conditions in a British town. For example, toys are not regarded as an integral part in the training of young children—this is not to say that they don't have them, but they are given as a special treat, and may be regarded as a temporary diversion only; the range is limited and rather unsophisticated— balls, marbles, 'Matchbox' cars, trumpets and drums are more common than constructional toys; tricycles and pedal cars figure in outdoor play; girls have dolls, often big, expensive types that offer less scope for dressing, putting to bed and generally knocking around than the less pretentious kinds. Constructional toys, puzzles and toys demanding the use of some skill are not often bought. Books are not generally bought for young children—the idea of a 'picture book', for looking at rather than reading is unfamiliar, though the big cheap colouring books from Woolworths are bought by Sikh mothers, and older brothers and sisters are likely to have crayons, pencils and supplies of scrap paper, all of which is good scribbling material. In the Punjab, children improvise toys from any available scraps, and this resourcefulness is found amongst British Sikh children to some extent; younger children are allowed to make use of all sorts of domestic things as temporary toys— in fact, the 'whole vocation' or a good part of the play-life of Sikh infants is imitation, a fact which is recognized by Sikh parents and traditional 'child psychology'. The period of infancy—*bala*, (from birth to the coming of second teeth) is regarded as one when the children are occupied mainly in exploring and imitating the world about them, so mother gives them a little dough to make *chapattis*, pots of water to pour, handfuls of pulses to make 'dinner' with. Rather older children begin imitating the social and and ritual life of their elders—playing at weddings is a favourite pastime, acting incidents in traditional stories their parents have told them, and re-enacting the ceremonies of seasonal festivities; also, just playing at families, with different children (girls and little boys) playing the roles of grandmother, mother and so on in daily life. These children often develop a wickedly accurate skill in mimicry. The imitative play that absorbs the little child gives training in practical skills—a child with mother's box of buttons to sort can develop a range of categories of size, shape and colour—and there is a simple transition at an early age from imitative play to actually helping mother or father in domestic tasks (in the traditional society of India, of course, this is how the child learns his 'family trade'). Similarly, ritual and play-acting have an important part in developing the child's ability to play social roles and to manage—both by controlling and by expressing —his or her emotions.

As children grow older, they become more aware of the constraints placed on their behaviour by the family with whom they live; in particular, they become more subject to the discipline of their fathers. Discipline is regarded largely as the self-restraint necessary for comfortable life within the family, rather than the arbitrarily imposed will of the elders in the family—punishments are not normally harsh or frequent: cases of cruelty in Sikh families here are rare, and arise from abnormal emotional disturbance in a parent. The Sikhs place a high value on truthfulness, at any rate amongst members of a family; if a child's relations with his parents are strained in any circumstance, he is most likely to be punished on the grounds that he has lied to them. Boys in particular are very leniently treated; where there is only one boy in a family he is likely to be 'spoiled', having his own way all the time. The youngest child in a family is generally the recipient of most indulgent treatment, too.

The imitative play of the young child, as we have mentioned, develops into 'helping' the parents in the house; quite young children are entrusted with a fair amount of responsibility. Girls tend to have a heavier load of duties than boys; this is probably the case in the Punjab, and in Britain there is not the possibility of boys learning their fathers' trades—helping on the farm or in the workshop. Girls help with the preparation of food, serving food to their fathers and other men of the family, washing and mending clothes, and keeping the house clean. In the Punjab, a girl is expected to acquire a range of domestic skills by the time she is marriageable, so that specimens of her work can be offered as part of her dowry. In Britain, they are still learning these skills, though using electric cookers, washing machines and sewing machines.[1]

Boys can help their fathers in 'do it yourself' activities in the home; many of the fathers are interested in machinery or in making things, and their children develop skills as they 'help' them.

At the same time, the older child makes less demands than an infant does on adults for companionship, and turns to the company of other children. The Sikh child will select playmates from circles of children with whom he has contact—firstly, his own brothers and sisters, then, other Sikh children living in the same street or nearby (including, possibly, some children related through the extended family); there will also be other Punjabi-speaking children, Hindus or Muslims—to the young child, the social distinctions will not be significant, except that his parents' relations with these children's parents, while probably quite friendly, may not be as close as they are with other Sikhs. After these, are children in the neighbourhood who are not Punjabi-speaking—the English, West Indian, Irish and European. The friendship patterns of such children could usefully be studied in detail: they must vary considerably, depending on the child's ability to use English, the range of different nationalities in the street, the numbers of Punjabis in particular, and several other factors.

In schools, children who are in special classes to learn English stick together very much in the playground (especially, of course,

---

[1] Punjabi handicrafts are not as well-known overseas as the work of some other Indian states; however, the work of Punjabi women, done in their own homes, is often of a very high standard; methods and designs are highly regulated by local tradition, varying from one place to another, but characterized by bold, bright colours arranged in geometric patterns.

The classic piece of handwork, often given as a present or part of a dowry, is a *Phulkara*, a sheet of brightly coloured cotton (always a shade of red, from bright scarlet to brick) embroidered with multicoloured silk. They are used as bedspreads, covers for anything valuable in the house, and even as shawls. Other items of 'upholstery' are also delicately embroidered—cushions, pillows, cloths.

The Punjabi women's skill in needlework can be seen in the embroidery of their *kamiz*; the ankles of *shalwar* 'for best' are also embroidered. In the Punjab, they make many things needed about the house—heavy cotton rugs, baskets—and even such humble accessories as *nalas*, 'pyjama cords' for *shalwar* and *pajama* woven in bright colours, but there is little need for such handwork in Britain.

where the special class is situated in an 'annexe', some distance from the school). When they are placed in 'normal' classes, they are likely to be fairly isolated (this was, of course, one object of the Local Education Authority's 'dispersal' policy, to reduce the proportion of 'coloured' children in schools in certain neighbourhoods) —they may, at playtime, join Punjabi children from other classes, or they may form friendships with children in their own classes, but, because they live away from the school's neighbourhood, they are unlikely to maintain these friendships in any consistent way out of school. Where Sikh children have attended their neighbourhood school, they have formed more consistent friendship groups in and out of school, but these have been mainly all-Punjabi, even all-Sikh groups, except in areas where the number of Punjabi children in any single age-group is very small. Where there is a number of Sikh boys of similar age, the formation of a pre-adolescent 'gang' is a normal feature of play-life.

However, the importance of the family must again be emphasized—a child with two or three brothers and sisters may play only with them, and have little to do with other children in the neighbourhood, especially if there are few Punjabis.

The partial 'isolation' of many Sikh children, alone or in separate groups, can lead to limitation in their repertoire of games—boys, especially in special classes, seem in some cases to have nothing to do but play marbles with almost fanatical dedication. They like 'war games' of any kind as much as English boys, but such games require a stable group of friends who agree on the conventions; games of the 'Cowboys and Indians' type played by multi-racial groups are apt to bring to light tensions and misunderstandings, so are likely to be avoided. In chasing games, the conventions are more explicit, and Sikh children learn these from other children, including the elaborate counting-out ceremonies that can prove more interesting than the game itself (some Punjabi counting-out rhymes, remembered by older brothers and sisters, are used still when they play together). Trials of strength between individuals—running, swimming, wrestling—are liked, provided, again, that they don't expose tensions between groups divided on racial lines: the Sikh boys enjoy a 'friendly fight', and feel fairly well at ease they are with friends) at the public swimming baths, usi learned in school swimming lessons.

Other pastimes come and go with fashion. Ma a stalwart—Punjabi forms generally involve ge a small depression in the ground (a 'pog' in a English games of marbles are fairly s where agreement on 'rules' is quite pos by multi-racial groups. Sikh boys always and teachers are often required to adjudica tions of possession.

A game of skill that had practically died out in England has been revived to some extent by Punjabi immigrants—it was known in Yorkshire as 'Pig and stick' and by other names elsewhere ('Tip-cat', etc.) and in Punjabi it is *Guli danda*. It is played with a stick about two feet long and a tapered billet about three inches long. The player taps the billet with the stick to make it fly up, then tries to strike it, hitting it as far as he can (the billet is the *guli*, the stick the *danda*).

'Integration' is, of course, relatively straightforward in organized games where the rules are agreed on and skills are developed in school under adult supervision; Sikh boys join in street and playground games of football and cricket—some of their older brothers may play in teams, such as the 'Indian Stars' who have played in the local league against club and works teams since 1969; they have done very well in six-a-side contests.[1] The cult of the local football team is something much more 'tribal'; so far, Sikh boys have not attended football matches in great numbers, though they take as much interest as other boys in televised football matches and there is a group of dedicated Town fans, most 'Indian Stars' players, who go to home games at Leeds Road.

The traditional chasing and wrestling games of the Punjab, such as *Kabbadi and Kho-kho*[2] have not been played very much by immigrant children here, so their British-born younger brothers have not learned these games; Indian organizations elsewhere in Britain have occasionally organized sports festivals where these games have been played, so it is possible that they might be revived, but such a revival would be self-conscious and 'artificial'.

Girls and boys do play one Punjabi game that is exciting and simple enough for other children to have picked it up in some cases: this is *Pittu* (sometimes, *Garm pittu*). It is usually played by two pairs of players; four stones are piled in a little tower; one

[1] Hockey is the speciality of the Sikhs, who form the backbone of India's national teams; it is played all over the Punjab by boys on any available piece of waste ground, with knotty branches for sticks (*haki*) and stones or balls of rag. There is little encouragement for hockey in this part of Britain, though older Sikh boys do play hockey at some youth clubs. However, soccer is becoming very popular, and the bigger boys who came from the Punjab have memories of playing in bare feet; on the hard, grassless ground they develop skill in ball control and play an open, passing game with little physical contact.

[2] *Kabbadi*: played by two teams on a rectangular 'court' rather smaller than a badminton court. One boy from one team crosses the centre-line and tries to touch a boy on the other side; they run and dodge within their half of the area; after touching an opponent he tries to get back across the centre-line, while his opponent prevents him by wrestling with him. From the time the attacker crosses the centre-line, he has to keep saying *'Kabbadi kabbadi'*; he only scores a point if he can touch an opponent and get back across the centre-line without running out of breath.

Kho Kho: played by two teams. One team sit in a row, the players facing alternate ways, except for the one at the head who remains standing and is the 'chaser'. Opponents, three at a time, run up and down the line escaping from the chaser; they are allowed to dodge through the line, but the 'chaser' may not. He, however, touch a seated player saying *'Kho'*—that player starts chasing on the other side of the line, and the first 'chaser' sits down.

player throws the ball to knock down the tower—if he succeeds, he and his partner must build it again before their opponents can retrieve the ball and hit one of them with it; points are notched up each time a tower is successfully rebuilt.

Girls' games are likely to involve agility rather than physical strength, and have less likelihood of 'friendly' conflict becoming 'unfriendly'; on the other hand, the conventions are even more complex, and present a problem even to a child of English parents who move from a different district. A good many English games have Punjabi counterparts which older sisters may have gone on playing—so Sikh girls may know alternative English and Punjabi rhymes for counting-out, skipping, hopscotch, 'Oranges and Lemons', 'Lucy Locket', 'In and out the houses', 'Cat and mouse', 'I like coffee' and so on. Nursery and Infant Schools can do a valuable job just teaching the lyrics, rules and conventions that are locally observed in children's games to those whose parents and older brothers and sisters may not be able to.

The lore of the juvenile peer group is rich and time-honoured; the Sikh child will be at a disadvantage if he is not *au fait* with it. Jokes, such as those involving rhyming words ('Say knife and fork') may be a problem to a bilingual child, making him an easy butt for teasing. Of course, there is similar lore amongst Punjabi children; they may learn from older brothers and sisters jokes, riddles,[1] parodies and 'naughty' stories in their mother tongue. Children's lore, like the songs, dances, ring-games and stories learnt in childhood, is a living and vigorous expression of a community's culture. Children of a minority culture with traditions of its own are in an ambivalent position; teachers must try to understand the culture of the home in all its manifestations, and the way in which Sikh parents are trying to bring up their children, if they are to be able to help these children to overcome the difficulties arising from this ambivalence, and indeed to benefit from the unusual breadth of their experience.

[1] I used to kiss the old man's whiskers—
Now I don't even look at him.
Who is he? (a mango stone)

4 Religion and *Dharam*

There is a fair amount of literature available in English now on the subject of the Sikh religion; some of this literature should certainly be studied by anyone working with Sikh children in Britain. They will be gratified to discover that it is not a mass of superstition, idolatry, dark practices or meaningless taboos. Its starting point is a very refined and elevated conception of the Absolute, an idea explored in the profound poetry of Guru Nanak's *Japji Saheb* (the first portion of the *Guru Granth Saheb*, recited as morning prayer by devout Sikhs). It has a rigorous metaphysical framework which excludes speculation—there is no great interest in the 'after life', and miracles are discounted; the emphasis of its teaching is on man's role, as an individual and as a member of human society, and he is held responsible for working out his own salvation. Sikh morality requires that man should play an active part in society, raising a family and doing useful work; he is expected to take an active part in democratic institutions, and to take responsibility for improving the lot of his fellows to the best of his ability. Idolatry and ritual is disliked, and the idea of a priest or any person in a special 'superior' role is rejected. This religion has something in common with the more rational forms of Protestant Christianity—particularly the social conscience, the emphasis on individual responsibility, the dislike of ritual and ostentation and the uncompromising egalitarianism. But Sikhs would not accept the necessity of a 'Saviour' in the Christian sense —the role of Guru is quite different; Guru Gobind Singh said:

> Those who call me God shall fall into the depths of Hell. Greet me as God's humble servant only. Do not have any doubts that this is true. (*Bachiter Natak*, MX, 6:32.)

But we must ask how far an understanding of the teachings of the Sikh Gurus is helpful or necessary for a teacher who wants to understand Sikh children living in twentieth-century Britain. How important is religion in their lives, and the lives of their parents?

In the first place, we may need to revise our understanding of what is meant by 'religion'. We think of religion as, firstly, a set of beliefs of a metaphysical kind that a Church's members are expected to agree on and accept—the 'background' books on the Sikh religion outline a corresponding set of beliefs elicited from the *Guru Granth Saheb*; secondly, we assume that the people who subscribe to a particular set of beliefs will try to conform to certain rules, taking Communion, going to Confession, reading the Bible daily, as the case may be. These we distinguish as 'religious' customs, and can see a difference between these and 'social' customs, such as the conventions of 'good manners'. When we discuss matters like the food or dress habits of immigrant families, we sometimes try to draw a similar distinction between 'social' and 'religious' customs. Such a distinction is meaningless to a Sikh, at least until he is influenced by Western culture or education. The world is described in the *Guru Granth Saheb* as a 'region of duty' (*Dharam*, Sanskrit *Dharma*, 'That which holds everything together'), and everything in it is fulfilling its *Dharam*. Man's *Dharam* is to live in society, raising a family, helping his fellows, trying to free himself of instincts of greed, fear, anger and so on so as to achieve calmness of mind and a clear conscience. Everything that he does is a significant part of his *Dharam*. So, eating a healthy diet, keeping clean, dressing correctly and so on, are important; to an unsophisticated Sikh they are probably more important than subscribing to a set of beliefs. Certainly duty to the family and community, including the maintenance of their traditions, is essentially a religious *Dharam*.

To return to our question, how important is religion in the life of the Sikhs? Without doubt, it is conspicuous in Sikh homes—pictures of the Gurus, and of events in their lives and places associated with them, decorate the walls of nearly all Sikh homes. These are usually tradesmen's calendars, from Indian shops in the neighbourhood or from friends or relations in India; they are seldom works of art by any standard of taste, crudely coloured and modelled, presumably derived, at several removes, from the sophisticated though highly conventional work of artists at the courts of Sikh Maharajahs; however, they are a distinctive feature of the home environment of Sikh children—they must be important elements in their developing imagination, and the stories they illustrate (assuming that these are explained to them) are factors in their early emotional and social growth.

Religious symbols are also used ornamentally, though less commonly amongst Sikhs than amongst Muslims (whose religious and cultural traditions make more use of floral and calligraphic designs, less of figurative art). Words or phrases in ornamental *Gurmukhi* script used as wall plaques, and occasionally painted on front doors and such places—the commonest is formed of the first two letters of the *Guru Granth Saheb*, the initials *Ik Onkar*

(੧੬ 'The Absolute is One'); other words used for the Absolute in the *Guru Granth Saheb* are also featured in illuminated script—*Satnam*, *Waheguru*, *Satguru Prasad* ('True Word', 'Great Guru', 'Grace of the True Guru'). Another symbol that features on calendars, books and artefacts, and is sometimes worn as a badge on the turban or lapel, is the collection of weapons which appears in black on the yellow *Nishan Saheb*,[1] the banner that flies over every *Gurdwara*. It consists of a *khanda* (the broad, double edged knife used in the Sikh initiation ceremony, *khande di pahal*), a *chakri* round it (a sharp edge steel discus), flanked by two *dilwars* crossed (scimitars).

The young Sikh will take such things as these for granted, as part of his home environment; as he grows older, he will realize that like his long hair, his steel bangle, or the way he greets his parents, '*Sat Sri Akal*' they are distinctive belongings of his own community, things which other children don't have; they will be starting-points in his awareness of being a Sikh. There may be more essential things associated with religion about the house, though they will be less conspicuous to a young child—for example, prayer books. The *Guru Granth Saheb* is a very big book, about five times the length of the Bible; moreover, it is held in great respect, and anyone who has a copy in his house has to set aside a room for it, where it can be solemnly installed and kept with great care (it has to be in a place where no-one is likely to walk above it, for example on the floor above).[2] For these reasons, relatively few families have the complete text in the house. But prayer-books do not have to be treated with such reverence, though they are generally wrapped in a clean cloth and kept carefully. They contain the *Nitnem* (Daily prayers), that is the *Japji Saheb*, *Rehiras* (evening) and *Sohila* (bed-time prayers), the *Jap Saheb*,

---

[1] It is the symbol of the Khalsa, the brotherhood of baptized Sikhs (see p. 47). It can also be in yellow or white on a blue field.

[2] One cannot overstate the importance of the *Guru Granth Saheb*. It is regarded as the embodiment of light in the same way as a human Guru. The Word (*Bani*, 'Logos') is the means by which the Absolute is made manifest:

> As the lotus flower
> does not drown in the pool,
> As the duck
> is not made wet by the pond—
> As the flower thrusts upwards,
> As the duck swims,
> So, with the mind intent
> Upon the Word of the Guru (*Gurbani*),
> One can safely cross
> the great sea of life—
> Repeating the Holy Name (*Sat Nam*),
> Living in aloneness,
> utterly intent
> upon the Alone;
> In a life of worldly hopes,
> purifying the mind
> of worldly desires.
>
> (*Sidh Gosht, Ramkali*, MI, p. 938.)

and other extracts from the *Gurbani* for various occasions; there may also be the full texts of some important long poems from the *Guru Granth Saheb*, usually in separate books—such as the *Asa di Var* of Guru Nanak and the *Sukhmani Saheb* of Guru Arjun.

A sense of the religious background to everyday life is maintained by pious Sikhs in day-to-day observances. These derive primarily from instructions of Guru Ram Das in the *Granth Saheb*:

> He who would call himself a Sikh of the True Guru
> Should rise early in the morning and contemplate the Name.
> In the early hours of the morning, he should rise and bathe,
> And cleanse his soul in a tank of nectar.
> As he repeats the Name the Guru taught him,
> He washes away the sins of his soul.
> Then at dawn he should sing the hymns of the Guru.
> Throughout the business of the day,
> He should hold in his heart the Name.
> He that repeats the Name with every breath
> Such a Sikh is indeed dear to the Guru.
> The Sikh that wins the favour of the Lord
> Has received the gift of the Lord's Name from the Guru.
> Nanak seeks to kiss the dust under the feet of such a Sikh.
> Who utters the Name and inspires others to do so!
>
> *(Gavri Var, MIV, p. 305.)*

A Sikh is supposed to rise about an hour before dawn, take a bath, and recite the *Japji Saheb*[1]—if he cannot recite it, he simply repeats '*Satnam Waheguru*' ('The True Name of the Great Guru', a name of God) enough times to concentrate his mind and clear it of distractions.[2] In England, an early morning cold bath is less attractive than it is in India, and few Sikh homes at present have 'instant' hot water systems, so there is a strong discouragement to piety in this respect. Seriously, the majority of Sikhs in Britain have abandoned these observances, though I know a fair number of pious men—and women—who pray regularly. They usually pray standing up, or sitting, but people in a hurry may recite their prayer as they go about their work. After bathing, but before eating breakfast, a pious Sikh is supposed to read a lesson (*Hukm*) from the *Guru Granth*, either selecting a page at random, or reading through from beginning to end, a few *Shabads* each day. The evening prayers, *Rehiras* at sunset and *Sohila* at bed-time, are

---

[1] The *Jap Saheb* and certain *Swayyas*, all by Guru Gobind Singh, are also used as morning prayers.

[2] The Gurus preached against vain repetition of meaningless *mantras*, but recommended *Nam simran*—recollection of the Word—as a means of concentrating the mind, reminding one of the Absolute, removing cravings and anxieties and producing a calm, detached frame of mind in tune with the Absolute. This is a very difficult and sophisticated idea, a kind of mystical detachment amongst the distractions of daily life; for most Sikhs, repetition of the Name of the Great Guru (*Satnam Waheguru*) is a simple exercise in concentrating the mind. The significance of *Nam Simran*, the Sikh form of prayer and meditation, can best be understood by studying Guru Nanak's *Debate with the Yogis* (*Sidh Gosht, Ramkali*, MI, pp. 938-947.)

not recited by so many Sikhs even in India, though many pious people use them, and the same applies here. Young children are not expected to pray in this way even in pious families, though they may be taught to say '*Satnam Waheguru*'.

Children of relatively pious parents may often hear them use this phrase (or simply '*Waheguru*') as they go about their work. For example, when a woman begins making roti, she may say '*Waheguru*'. When someone sneezes or yawns involuntarily, he will do likewise. Prayer is likely to be resorted to in times of trouble, such as illness. Sikhs (especially women) who have become depressed or otherwise emotionally disturbed by the strains of migration and life in Britain, apparently find comfort in reciting *Gurbani*—Guru Arjun's *Sukhmani Saheb* ('Song of Peace', a remarkable description of the state of the human mind when perfect calm and equanimity is achieved) is a favourite at such times, as are several *slokas* (brief, pithy verses) of Guru Tegh Bahadur that are on a similar theme, e.g.:

> Not cast down by sorrow
> nor over-elate in joy;
> Aloof from the power
> of pride, greed and coveting
> Such a man, saith Nanak,
> is the image of God.
>
> > (*Slok*, 13 MIX, p. 1,326.)

> Happiness and prosperity find many friends
> but adversity and sorrow have none.
> Saith Nanak, 'Ponder on the Beloved, my soul—
> even in the bitterness of death he is thy true Saviour!'
>
> > (*Slok*, 32 MIX, p. 1,427.)

The religion of the Sikhs began as a protestant movement against superstition and idolatry, and the Sikhs are certainly free of the grosser superstitions one sees amongst other communities in India. They do not suffer from the belief in pervasive supernatural powers, evil influences or ghosts that afflicts many people from tradition-bound societies. Idolatry is certainly alien to them, though pictures of the Gurus are sometimes used as a focus of attention when praying; these may be garlanded with flowers or streamers, and *agarbattis* (joss sticks) are sometimes burnt before them, though these practices are strictly not permitted.

On the other hand, many practices which the Gurus condemned have persisted. The very idea that prayer, like a magic formula, can alter events or circumstances was explicitly condemned by the Gurus as contrary to the idea of an omnipotent 'Divine Will'. Astrology and other forms of divination were ridiculed by the Gurus:

Without the True Guru there is utter darkness,
and he is a common fool
who regards certain days in the lunar or solar calendars as
auspicious.

(Rag Bilawal, MIII.)

But there are Sikh astrologers, some practising in Britain and
advertising in Punjabi newspapers. Some families obtain horoscopes for their children when they are born, and these are often
consulted, especially when a compatible marriage has to be
arranged. Astrologers are also consulted about auspicious days,
say for a wedding ceremony, for undertaking a new business, or
moving into a new house. Certain times of the year are considered
especially auspicious, particularly the 'light' half of the month of
Magh (Capricorn), and days of the week have particular strengths
or weaknesses—if you have a new ring, you should put it on on
Monday, but new clothes are better put on on Wednesday. One
comes across residual belief in magic amongst children—in
charms, bewitching and the 'Evil Eye'—probably to be taken no
more seriously than a small child's belief in fairies. Like traditional
English beliefs, they are relics in child-lore of beliefs once widely
held, of sinister importance, but now largely forgotten. None of
these superstitions are universally, or even widely held amongst
Sikhs in Britain, and within the Punjab, details vary from place
to place, even family to family; the Sikh in Britain is as likely
to believe in 'luck' as his English neighbours—hardly any more so.

The religious and social life of an émigré Sikh community
centres on the *Gurdwara*, and it is important to appreciate its
function. The Gurus made it clear that attendance at communal
worship is a necessary part of the spiritual life of a Sikh:

Sat Sangat (the Holy Congregation) is the school of the
True Guru.
There we learn to love him and appreciate his greatness.

(Var Kanra, MIV.)

Bhai Gurdas equated the *Sangat* with the inspired person of a
Guru:

The Supreme Being, the Perfect One,
the True Guru lives in *Sat Sangat*.
Sat Sangat is just like the Guru,
it is filled with love of the Immortal.

(Bhai Gurdas Var, 13, 14.)

It is far more of a social centre than, say, a Mosque, for it is not
just a place where people go to pray, but the accepted meeting
place of the community; moreover, women and children attend, in
fact, it is a family centre, certainly unlike a Mosque, and Christian

churches are hardly similar, though some public-spirited clergy might wish they were. Technically, a *Gurdwara* is the 'Home of the Guru', that is, a place where the *Guru Granth Saheb* is installed —thus, a room in a private house may, as we have described, serve as a *Gurdwara*; but it must be public—that is, anyone who wishes to enter at any time must be admitted, lodging for travellers and a free kitchen must be provided for anyone who wants, and it serves as a centre for social, charitable and educational work. Attendance at the *Gurdwara* is an indication, if not of the importance of religion in the life of the Sikhs, at least of their sense of being Sikhs and wishing to associate with a distinct community.

There is a *Granthi* or *Bhai* who acts as caretaker, and is also skilled in reciting *Gurbani*; he has to keep the *Gurdwara* clean and admit any visitors. He recites the daily prayers at the appropriate times, and anyone can join him in these; people can come in at any time to pray. In fact, the number of people who visit on weekdays is quite small, though there are some who go regularly, mainly women.

A *Sangat* is held on Sunday; this is an 'assembly', for purposes of worship, receiving religious instruction from respected members of the community, and discussing matters of communal interest. There is no special reason why it should take place on Sundays. The Gurus taught that all days are equally important. The Sikhs simply use the local holiday—*Gurdwaras* in the Persian Gulf States hold their *Sangats* on Friday for the same reason; in India, Sunday is still a weekly holiday, and so the *Gurdwaras* there expect larger *Sangats* on that day. Attendance at the weekly *Sangats* in Huddersfield is usually quite substantial: on a miserable day in winter, with no special occasion to celebrate, the congregation is seldom less than a hundred (as people come and go during the course of the *Sangat*, it is difficult to give an exact figure, but the maximum number is usually present between 12.30-1.30). On such days, the preponderance of women over men is noticeable, sometimes as much as 70-30. If there is interesting business —a festival, a wedding, or some important matter to be discussed —the numbers will be much greater, the proportion of men especially. The largest *Sangat* so far was on the occasion of Guru Nanak's 500th aniversary in 1969, when the number of people who attended some part of the proceedings was little under 1,000, about 750 taking part in the procession that formed the climax. Other festivals and weddings have been attended by 400 or more. The present *Gurdwara* is not big enough to hold such numbers: more than about 180 becomes uncomfortable.

In effect, a Sikh family, at least mother and children, are likely to attend the *Gurdwara* on a Sunday if they are not doing anything else—such as visiting relatives; they will certainly try to attend on major festivals, and will be sure to attend weddings of friends and relatives, when they have to choose a name for a new baby, and on other family occasions. Sikh mothers who go out to work, though, are often too tired or busy to attend.

The *Gurdwara* depends on voluntary contributions for its income. Anyone entering is required to bow to the floor before the *Guru Granth Saheb*, and make some offering, which is usually a token sum of money, but ingredients for *Karah Prashad*, cloths to cover the *Guru Granth* and other things needed in the *Gurdwara* are also offered. More substantial sums of money are handed over to the treasurer against a receipt, and announced towards the end of the *Sangat* (though really donations are supposed to be anonymous). Contributions are quite generous, amounting to twenty pounds and upwards each Sunday, indicating 75p–£1 per family.

Gurdwaras vary in layout, and those in Britain have been adapted to the type of building they are in. A common type in Punjabi villages resembles a mosque (some are converted mosques) with a courtyard where the people sit (under awnings in hot weather), facing a rectangular building along one wall of the courtyard. This corresponds to the 'prayer-hall' of a mosque, and usually has three arches, the *Guru Granth Saheb* being installed inside the middle arch, while singers, preachers and temple officials occupy the two sides. *Gurdwaras* in Britain seem to derive their internal layout from this plan (rather than from those, including the *Durbar Saheb* at Amritsar and most other large ones, where the *Guru Granth Saheb* is on the central axis, near to the middle of a rectangular building). In the Hudderfield *Gurdwara*, the *Guru Granth* is on cushions on a *diwan* (platform) under a carved wooden canopy half way along one of the longer walls of a rectangular room (in fact, it is the upstairs part of an old house with all internal walls removed). When it is not being read, the *Guru Granth* is kept shut, under silk cloths (*ramala*) which are donated from time to time by members of the congregation. People enter through a door in a corner on the opposite side, and, after making obeisance to the *Guru Granth Saheb*, they sit, women to the left and men to the right (of one facing the *diwan*), in a semi-circle leaving room for people to come and go. To the right of the *diwan* is a dais where singers and temple officers sit. They have microphones connected to a powerful loudspeaker above the wooden canopy, which has strip lights attached to it to shine on the *Guru Granth*. The only other furniture is cupboards for musical instruments and loudspeaker controls. The canopy is decorated with flowers and streamers, and this decoration is extended throughout the room for festivals. There are posters and pictures on the walls of events in the lives of the Gurus, like those seen in Sikh homes.

The *Granthi* ('reader', *not* a priest in any sense) sits behind the

Guru waving a *chauri* (a yak's tail fly-whisk, a sign of respect). This post can be occupied by any man or woman who is baptized Sikh and able to recite *Gurbani*, and there are several members of a community of 1,200 or so who can and do act as *Granthi*, relieving the full-time *Granthi* who is employed to look after the *Gurdwara*.

A *Sangat* can commence when five or more people are present. The *Granth Saheb* is opened at random and whatever is found on that page recited by the *Granthi*, starting at the top left-hand corner of the page (or on the previous page when a *Shabad* runs over more than one page); this is called a *hukm* (command, lesson), or *wak* (reading chosen at random). At a normal Sunday *Sangat*, this is generally done about 10.30 a.m. After this, there is *Kirtan*, singing of *Shabads* (hymns) from the *Guru Granth*. The hymns of Guru Gobind Singh (in *Dasm Granth*) and the *Viyakhaya* (exposition) of Bhai Nand Lal and Bhai Gurdas may also be sung in *Kirtan*, by *ragis* (musicians)—there are professional *ragis* in India, but in villages, and amongst communities abroad, anyone who can play an instrument and knows how to sing *Shabads* is invited. The contents of the *Guru Granth Saheb* (except the *Japji Saheb*) are all lyrical and intended to be sung to various classical *ragas* (modes; the contents of the *Granth Saheb* are arranged according to *raga*). The music of the *Gurdwaras* is obviously related to Punjabi secular music, but it is more bound by traditional forms. It is, however, very vigorous and emotional. It is generally accompanied on the *tabla* (drums), *dhola* (side-drums) and harmonium (the small, box-type, which has, unfortunately, superseded more melodious wind and stringed instruments). This *Kirtan* is interspersed with *Ketha* (exposition) ranging from brief explanation of the contents of a stanza to full-scale sermons. These may be delivered by any respected member of the community. Any Sikh, man or woman, who wishes may sing a *Shabad* or other religious song, recite a poem or relate a story from Sikh history, and children are encouraged to take part. All speeches and recitations are begun and ended with Guru Gobind Singh's salutation, '*Waheguruji ka Khalsa: Sri Waheguruji Ki Fateh*' ('The Great Guru's *Khalsa*: The Great Guru's Victory'). There is virtually no 'congregational' singing, though people may join in spontaneously when a familiar hymn is sung. Thus, the proceedings are largely unstructured—there is no prescribed ritual or 'service' to be followed; the programme is arranged by the 'Stage Secretary', an elected official who receives requests from anyone wishing to say or recite anything and allots time to them. Of course, when a festival is being celebrated, it is likely that people will sing or speak about the occasion, and there are *Shabads* that relate to particular occasions such as Guru Nanak's *Baramaha* (*Rag Tukhari*, MI, pp. 1,107-1,100, a series of stanzas for each month of the year). When the *ragis* have finished their *Kirtan*, and everyone who wishes has sung or spoken, announcements are made by elected officials of the *Gurdwara Prabhandak* (Management) Committee, principally the Secretary and Treasurer—business discussions, elections and so are normally left till after the *Sangat* has been ended, but speeches on religious matters in the course of a *Sangat* are apt to drift into communal politics.

There are set procedures for closing a *Sangat*, generally about 1.30-2.00 on a normal Sunday. The first five stanzas and the last from a hymn of Guru Amar Das known as the *Anand Saheb* (*Rag Ramkali*, MIII, pp. 917-922, a remarkable song of religious ecstasy) are usually sung, then all the *Sangat* stand up and sing a verse in praise of the Gurus and the *Granth Saheb* and afterwards a *Granthi* recites the *Ardas*—this is generally called 'The Sikh Prayer', though it is in fact addressed to the Sikhs; it is an expanded form of an exhortation by Guru Gobind Singh to the *Khalsa*, reminding them to remember the teachings of the Gurus, the sufferings of Sikh martyrs, and the words of the *Guru Granth Saheb*. All bow to the floor and stand again to recite a verse in which they undertake to remember these instructions, and end with the Sikh war-cries: '*Raj karega Khalsa, akhi na re koe*' ('The *Khalsa* shall rule, there shall be no slaves!'), '*Bole so nihal, Sat Sri Akal*' ('Who hears this shall be saved—Truth is the Eternal Lord'). All bow towards the *Guru Granth*, then sit again while another *wak* (random reading from the *Guru Granth Saheb*) is taken.

Throughout the session of the *Sangat*, people are coming and going; not many will stay for the full three hours or more. Children are allowed to run out and play when they get bored, and they come in and go out quite freely; babies are brought in by their mothers, and given milk or dummies if they cry. The atmosphere is that of a jolly family occasion—there is none of the hushed solemnity required in a church. The children are not expected to pay much attention to the songs and sermons; it is not expected that they will understand much of what is going on, though they are trained to bow to the Guru and make an offering when they enter, and to take part in the *Ardas*; as they get older, they might learn songs or poems to recite, and are duly rewarded by their parents if they do this well in public (they generally learn these things in the *Gurdwara* classes, which we shall describe later). For them it is mainly an opportunity to meet friends (it has this function for their parents, too, of course), and it is another part of their life that is 'different' from what other children do on Sunday, another thing that teaches them that they are—in this case very visibly—members of a distinctive community.

The *Sangat* ends with distribution of *Karah Prashad*; *Karah* is a kind of halwa made of semolina (*sujji*), milk, butter and sugar, flavoured with cinnamon (*dalchini*) and other spices; it is mixed at the *Gurdwara* during the singing of *Anand Saheb*, the ingredients being brought by members of the *Sangat* (especially any who have cause for thanksgiving—birth of a child, a wedding, etc.), stirred with a *khanda* (a broad, double-edged knife), and given to everyone present as an expression of equality, social solidarity and rejection of caste exclusiveness. Sometimes, sweets or fruit are brought by a member of the *Sangat* to be given to the children.

On special occasions, there is a full-scale meal served down-stairs, from the *Guru da Langar* ('The Guru's Kitchen'); this is an important institution for the Sikhs—the *Gurdwaras* of bigger Sikh communities in Britain serve *Langar* every week, and the great *Gurdwaras* in India have daily, even 24-hour *Langars*. The meal is simple, consisting generally of *dal* (pulse of any kind), *sabzi* (vegetables), *dehi* (yogurt generally spiced with pieces of pasta or vegetable added) or *acchar* (pickle) and *roti* (unleavened bread), with *kher* (rice pudding) or some other sweet dish to follow, and water to drink. Like the *Karah Prashad*, this communal meal is an assertion of communal solidarity; it also symbolizes the charitable duties of a Sikh community. *Gurdwaras* have the duty of providing food and lodging for anyone in need; even a small one in Britain has arrangements for this, and it is sometimes used by Sikhs visiting the town if they cannot for any reason lodge with friends or relatives—no charge is made, though visitors are expected either to make some offering or do some domestic work.

Hospitality in their own homes is regarded by Sikhs as part of their *Dharam* or duty: a guest, even if he is unexpected, receives every attention. All work ceases, and no effort is spared to make him comfortable—this is thought to bring great credit and blessings to the host; stories about divine messengers disguising themselves as travellers are a feature of Punjabi folklore, as in many other parts of the world.

Generosity in other respects is also a characteristic; collections of money are organized for a variety of reasons, besides the regular offerings at the *Gurdwara*, and individuals make it a matter of pride to contribute substantial sums—a pound, two, five or even ten are quite common individual contributions to any collection. Collections organized recently amongst local Sikhs (not necessarily through the *Gurdwara*) have been for relief of refugees in Bengal, fighting apartheid, publishing books on Sikh religion for children, buying new premises for the *Gurdwara*, and for many other purposes. Especially generous donations to Temple funds are made by families at times of weddings, birth of sons and so on.

In the Punjab, the year is punctuated by a succession of festivals and commemorations, of varying importance. There are no days when a holiday is compulsory (like the *Eids* of the Muslims) nor are there any times of fasting (like *Ramzan*; fasting, simply as a religious observance, was condemned by the Gurus as pointless and likely to lead to the sin of pride). In Britain, festivals are celebrated at the Gurdwara generally on the following Sunday. Major festivals are celebrated with an *Akand Path*: this is a continuous recitation of the entire *Guru Granth Saheb*.[1] It takes about 36 hours, with *Granthis* working in relays, so generally commences on Friday evening to finish on Sunday morning before the *Sangat*. While it is going on, a fair number of people come to sit and listen. On such occasions the *Sangat* may be prolonged, and it is likely that several children will have some recitations prepared. In the Punjab, important festivals are celebrated in processions, when the *Guru Granth Saheb* is carried through the streets on top of some vehicle, preceded by *Panch Piare* (warriors representing the 'Five beloved' followers of Guru Gobind Singh who volunteered to sacrifice their lives at his bidding) and guarded by warriors all with drawn swords. Such a procession was held in Huddersfield on the 500th anniversary of Guru Nanak in November 1969. But the fireworks, the funfairs and sideshows, the markets and gatherings that make these events high-spots in the life of Punjabi children cannot be re-created.

Some festivals are *Gurpurbs*, commemorating the births and deaths of the Gurus and important events in their lives. Some are celebrated more than others—most important seem to be the Martyrdom of Guru Arjun Dev (in *Jeth*), the Birthday of Guru Nanak (in *Katak*), the Martyrdom of Guru Tegh Bahadur (in *Maghar*), the Martyrdom of the two little sons of Guru Gobind Singh (in *Pokh*), the Birthday of Guru Gobind Singh (in *Pokh*).[2] There is a number of days that were celebrated anciently as seasonal festivals, with Hindu associations, but which became important for the Sikhs for special reasons—*Hola Mahalla* (in *Magh*, when *Nihang* warriors fight mock battles at Anandpur Saheb; it is the day after the Spring Equinox); *Baisakhi* (the first day of *Baisakh*, the Spring Harvest Festival in the Punjab; it was a day when representatives of all the Sikhs used to assemble before the Guru at Amritsar, and the day when Guru Gobind Singh established the *Khalsa*); *Diwali* (the new moon of *Katak*, the Winter Festival of Light, when Hindus celebrate the victory of Lord Rama and the generosity of Lakshmi, was also another 'assembly' day for the Sikhs).

[1] *Akand Path* is also performed by pious families (either by members of the families or *Granthis* commissioned by them) at times of great joy, sorrow or anxiety.

[2] The months of the Punjabi year are those of the N. Indian *Vikramjit* Era, corresponding roughly to the passage of the sun through the zodiac. The year begins when the sun enters Aries. The months, in Punjabi, are:

Chet (Aries), *Baisakh* (Taurus), *Jeth* (Gemini), *Asad* (Cancer), *Savan* (Leo), *Bhadon* (Virgo), *Asun* (Libra), *Katak* (Scorpio), *Maghar* (Sagittarius), *Pokh* (Capricorn), *Magh* (Aquarius), and *Phalgun* (Pisces).

The first day of each month is celebrated in *Gurdwaras* by singing Guru Nanak's 'Song of the Months' (*Baramaha Rag Tukhari*, MI, pp. 1,107-1,110). *Baisakhi* and *Maghi* are especially important 'firsts'. The new moon (*Masai*) is also celebrated, but not much in Britain.

These are the main festivals celebrated by Sikhs in Britain; there are numberless others celebrated in the Punjab, many of them local, for nowhere is far from some site associated with the life of one of the Gurus, and there are many other, more ancient celebrations which have marked the turning of the year since long before the Gurus, and these are celebrated at home or by village communities without any 'religious' ceremonies—*Tian, Karva Chouth, Dashera, Tikka, Lohri, Basant Panchmi* and many more.[1] There is no sign of any of these surviving here; the local festivities—Easter Eggs, fireworks, Father Christmas and so on have taken their place in the life of British Sikh children. Moreover, *Diwali* and *Baisakhi* are hardly 'celebrated' in many homes in any way that children would notice, so that Christmas plays a much bigger part in his life. Parents may simply not know the appropriate date each year, and (apart from lighting candles at *Diwali*) can hardly adapt the largely outdoor, communal ways of celebration of the Punjab to the sitting-room of an English house. Birthdays, an 'annual event' for British children, are not celebrated in the Punjab, but the custom is being widely adopted by Sikhs in England.

A feature of Indian life is the *Sadhu* or Holy Man, who travels from one temple to another, living on alms. Sikhs are forbidden to do this,[2] but there are a great many 'Saints' who travel about preaching, or else reside in one place, on the outskirts of a village. They may occupy a small cell attached to a *Gurdwara* (like a mediaeval anchorite), or sometimes the shrine or *samadhi* (cremation place) of an earlier saint, but many live in *pakka* houses in reasonable comfort. They may live in deep meditation, receiving offerings of food from pious villagers, but many are very active, serving as spiritual and practical advisers to villagers who consult them, and organizing communal activities such as schools or health centres. At Lopon (Ludhiana District), for example, one such saint has started a health centre and a women's college. At Rara Saheb (Ludhiana District) two saints have a fine colony with a school, orphanage, farm and many other amenities. Saints may even be active politicians—Sant Fateh Singh and Sant Chanan Singh dominated the Akali party and Punjabi politics in general during the 1960s.

Such saints keep in touch with their disciples overseas, and quite often undertake tours around the world, visiting the *Gurdwaras* of Sikh communities. The saint from Lopon is only one of many who have visited the Huddersfield *Gurdwara*. Such visits attract good congregations—often, to fit in with a travelling schedule, they hold

---

[1] There are no seasonal fasts observed by the Sikhs, and fasting on certain days, at particular stages of life or in order to obtain spiritual benefit was forbidden by the Gurus.

[2] Guru Amar Das said, 'a man whose mind is enlightened by the Guru remains a householder, doing his work without being "attached", controlling his desires'.

a *Sangat* on a weekday evening, but all who knew of the Saint when they were in India, and others who are interested, will attend. The Saint will deliver a sermon or perform *Kirtan*, and usually they accept generous contributions intended to defray their travelling expenses and support their philanthropic projects in India; occasionally, though, a Saint comes who refuses any gifts.

Thus a Sikh, as well as following the common tenets of his religion, may also owe spiritual allegiance to some living (or recently dead) Saint, either one who lived near his village or a famous one from further away. Saints may have only a few disciples, maybe only one, or they may command a vast following. In most cases, they remain orthodox Sikhs, and avoid the temptation to identify themselves as Gurus, but there are some heretical sects whose leaders are regarded by their followers as Gurus on a par with Guru Nanak and his successors. In Huddersfield, there are a few *Radhasoami Satsangis*, who owe allegiance to Master Charan Singh and his predecessors. This *Satsang* has an impressive colony at Beas (Amritsar District); its doctrines are an amalgam of Sikh and Yogic Hindu philosophy. Of course, this is unpopular with orthodox Sikhs, who also object to the 'personality cult' surrounding this Guru, which detracts from the respect that they feel should be reserved for the Ten Sikh Gurus and the *Guru Granth Saheb*. However, when Master Charan Singh visited London in 1970, he attracted enough devotees to fill Drury Lane Theatre on three successive afternoons. There are members of other heretical sects elsewhere in Britain, such as *Namdharis* in Leeds, but I don't know of any other in Huddersfield.

For adult immigrant Sikhs, visits by Saints are a link with life in the Punjab; for children, they must be something of a mystery —strange, wild-looking people who obviously create a great impression on their parents. We shall consider as we go along how important the Sikh child's vague ideas about the Punjab, his ancestral home, must be to him, but the question presents itself now, whether the Sikhs in Britain will have any specifically religious reasons for remembering the Punjab, any sense in the back of their minds of an ultimate return—like the Jew's longing for Jerusalem —or even a sense of a duty to go there, like the Muslim's compulsory *Hajj* to Mecca?

Pilgrimage is certainly not demanded; the Gurus frequently referred to this custom amongst Hindus and Muslims as an example of wasted effort:

> Shall we go to bathe at the pilgrim-places?
> No. Nam is the only sacred place of pilgrimage.
> The Holy of Holies is the contemplation of the Word
> that gives inner light and spiritual illumination
> > (*Rag Dhanasari*, MI, p. 687,
> > tr. Ranbir Singh, *The Sikh Way of Life*, p. 17.)

However, the fine *Gurdwaras* throughout the Punjab and in other parts of India, associated with important events in the lives of the Gurus, are visited by devout Sikhs, who wipe the dust from the threshold and spread it on their foreheads.[1] The most important is, of course, Amritsar—the *Durbar Saheb* (Golden Temple), the 'Pool of Nectar' (*Amrit-Sar*) itself, and the *Akal Takht*; certainly any Sikh will try to visit there at least once in his lifetime—he may bathe in the pool, and even preserve some of its water in a bottle to bring back to Britain, but he may be too sophisticated for such observances, and treat the visit as a great emotional experience without expecting any spiritual benefit from it. There are many other places with important associations—for example, Nankana Saheb (Talwandi), in Pakistan, the birthplace of Guru Nanak; the Pakistan Government generally allows parties of Sikh pilgrims to visit this shrine on Guru Nanak's Birthday, and charter flights were organized for this purpose from Britain in the anniversary year, 1969.

It seems likely that the young British Sikh will want to visit the Punjab and will be encouraged in this by his parents, but primarily as his 'family home', rather than as a 'national home' (Israel) or 'religious home' (Mecca); however, he will think of Amritsar as a wonderful place that he hears about in stories and sees in pictures (admittedly, Indian calendars make a wedding cake of the *Durbar Saheb*, ignoring its restrained proportions and delicate ornamentation) and it is probable that the desire to see this place will be added motivation. Moreover, if he does go, he will be welcomed by his relations and fellow visitors as a 'long lost son'. The village home, the farm to which his parents contribute so much money, the relations and friends whose photos decorate the 'best room' in Britain, will become 'real' to him and his sense of identity with Punjabi culture will be reinforced. This could have a profound effect on his attitudes and behaviour when he returns to Britain.

There is also the possibility that a Sikh in exile will want to return to the Punjab to die; again, there is no religious reason for this—Guru Arjun wrote in *Sukhmani Saheb* that one would not become free of sin just by arranging to die at some hallowed place, though it seems quite likely that some immigrant Sikhs will retire to their family homes when they are too old to work; whether their children will do likewise remains to be seen. When a Sikh dies, his body is washed and dressed with the Sikh symbols; after a short laying-out, when all the family pay their respects, elegies and suitable *shabads* are sung, and photos are often taken, the body is shrouded (in white for men, red for women), and taken for crema-

---

[1] 'Your servant seeks to kiss the dust under the feet of such a Sikh who utters the Name and inspires others to do so' (Gauri Var, MIV, p. 305, quoted above). Pious people do this even when entering a *Gurdwara* in Britain— the parts of *Gurdwaras* used for worship are kept so clean that the 'dust' is imaginary.

tion (*Bhog*). In India, after a period of mourning, varying from a few days to a couple of weeks, the ashes are either buried on the family land, or scattered in a river or pool—some places have come to be regarded as especially auspicious for scattering ashes, such as Kiratpur on the Sutlej, although this is superstition not approved by orthodox Sikhs. In Britain, some Sikhs who want the ashes of a deceased relative scattered on flowing water make arrangements for them to be scattered at sea (as it is illegal to scatter them on inland rivers). The women of the family and their friends and fellow-villagers weep, sing dirges, and put away all 'luxurious' items in the house during the period of mourning. Some Pakistani Muslims who die in Britain have been flown back to Pakistan for burial alongside their ancestors, but I have not heard of any Sikh's ashes being returned in this way.[1]

It seems reasonable to say, then, that religion, or at least religious observances, continues to play a fairly important part in the life of the Sikh immigrant parents, in ways which are likely to influence their children. How does religious consciousness develop in the Sikh child? We mentioned that, while there is a lot of verbal interaction between mother and young child, this relates mainly to the acquisition of practical skills and the interpretation of the physical environment; there is little attempt to explain or elaborate social behaviour or relationships. As the child grows older, we have described how he becomes increasingly subject to the disciplinary demands of the family-community. In effect, the growing child learns largely by imitation and example; things are not 'explained' to him—he does them because his mother and father do the same. In the Punjab, everyone with whom he would come in contact would do much the same, too, but the Sikh child in Britain must

---

[1] Extravagant mourning in the 'oriental manner' is not approved of; Bhai Sunder's *Sadd* (Elegy, *Rag Ramkali Sunder*, p. 923), often sung at Sikh funerals, asks 'Is it good to weep and wail when God adorns the (deceased) Guru with a role of honour?'

The bereaved are expected to find consolation in reading from the *Guru Granth*. The Sikh view of death is eloquently expressed in *Akal Ustat* of Guru Gobind Singh:

> As out of a single stream
> countless waves rise up
> and, being water, fall
> back in water again—
> so from God's form emerge
> alive and inanimate things,
> and, since they arise from Him,
> they shall fall in Him again. (*Akal Ustat*, 87, MX.)

But this absorption in the Absolute is the fate only of the perfectly enlightened *Brahm-giani*. Those that have not achieved *Mukti* (Sanskrit, *Moksha*, 'liberation') remain entangled in the material world—reincarnated, in effect:

> Who cherisheth not the Lord's Name
> They are unfortunate, they waste away their lives;
> They are made to go round from birth to birth,
> They are born only to die.
> (*Rag Maru*, MIV, trans. Ranbir Singh.)

soon realize that the majority of people he meets act in significantly different ways in certain respects—religious practices are a major area of such differences.

This presents a problem to the Sikh community. Religious teaching in the *Gurdwaras* was always limited to reading and reciting from the *Guru Granth Saheb*. The *Granthi* was accorded great respect as the man who could convey the words of the Guru (*Gurbani*) from the *Granth Saheb*. The child was introduced to the *Granthi*, giving him a small gift, and was taught the opening lines of the *Japji Saheb*, in a ceremony that inculcated reverence for the teacher (as 'agent' of the Guru) and for the *Granth Saheb*. There is no tradition of 'religious education' in the sense of explaining the religious and moral teachings of the Gurus and the historical facts about them. Children have been largely dependent on the example of their families and the store of information they could pass on—'religious education' was seen as the duty of the family. This has led to much emphasis on symbolic forms, such as the wearing of long hair, and superstitious practices and 'fairy stories' about the Gurus have been passed on as readily as religious or historical truths. Ultimately, it could mean that the majority of Sikhs will have little or no understanding about the fundamentals of their religion, for the language of the *Guru Granth Saheb* is archaic and difficult to understand without an interpreter, especially where it relates to important but complex ideas.

Young people are expected to conform to norms of social behaviour without questioning; their parents tending either to insist on rigid adherence to conventions and traditions, without trying to relate these to the world in which their children are growing up, or else being content to let them drift. It may be possible for first generation immigrants, who came to Britain as adults, to avoid coming to terms with British ways, simply by avoiding much contact with non-Sikhs and making as little change in their lives as possible. But, as their children become aware of other communities, they are likely to become less and less willing to conform; serious tensions are likely to develop between young and old.

The basic element in Sikh moral teaching is *sewa*, service done without desire for reward. In a symbolic form, it is the voluntary work willingly done at a *Gurdwara*—preparing and distributing *Karah Prasad*, and the free *Langar*, cleaning, mending, decorating, looking after the congregation's shoes, and so on. In daily life, it is an ideal of selfless service to the community, but above all doing one's duty (*Dharam*) in one's own family and immediate circle (the village-kin circle in the Punjab, the émigré community abroad). Thus there is stress on obligations to others and the values of group-membership rather than the value given in the west—at least by the liberal-educated protestant middle-classes—to individual initiative and personal independence.

Attempts have been made to balance the influence of the non-Sikh 'majority culture' by organizing classes for children at the *Gurdwara*. These are currently held on Saturday and Sunday afternoons, and are quite popular with the children, who are sympathetically taught and not driven too hard. But these classes concentrate mainly on the Punjabi language and script (which we shall consider later) and on learning by heart portions of the *Japji Saheb*, *Shabads* and religious poems; good learners have opportunities to recite what they have learnt at Sunday morning *Sangats*. The Sikh Missionary Society was formed in 1969 by some Sikh teachers in Gravesend who appreciated that this kind of teaching was not enough, and that there was a pressing need to reinterpret Sikh traditions and show young Sikhs how the Guru's teaching can provide answers even to the questions asked by children in our social environment; they have published some well-written books in English containing historical accounts of the Gurus' lives, avoiding obvious mythology, but using stories not involving miracles that illustrate moral teachings, and introducing simple translations of important passages of *Gurbani*. These booklets have been distributed free to children in all *Gurdwaras*, but they need to be read and discussed with the children by experienced teachers—and there are plenty of Sikhs teaching in British schools who ought to be able to serve in this way. If Sikh children are to have self-confidence and pride in being what they are, it will not be enough for them to keep their hair long and learn *Shabads* by heart—they will need to understand the spirit of the Sikh religion, especially those aspects of the Guru's teaching that are most relevant to the problems of living in a complex industrial society.

As things are, maintaining Sikh traditions is seen mainly in terms of 'symbolic affirmation'; the immigrants are quite willing to adopt 'British' ways in many respects, but, when they come up against hostility, or feel they are being unfairly treated, they react by affirming vehemently some distinct, symbolic feature of their ways of life, such as insisting on wearing long hair and turbans. A wise old Sikh in India put it to me nicely: 'If you tell the Sikhs they may build *Gurdwaras* all over England and you will help them, they may not do much about it; if you forbid them to build *Gurdwaras*, they will start building them straight away!'

A *pakka* Sikh is technically one who has received *Amrit* (nectar) at the ceremony *Khande di Pahal*, which is the Sikh alternative to the *Pahal* of the Sacred Thread by which young Brahmins are initiated. To take *Amrit*, a young Sikh is supposed to have reached an age of discretion, and nowadays this is commonly at about 18 years old, often when they are about to marry or after marriage, though older Sikhs tell me they were 'baptized' in this way when they were as young as 10 or 12. Even in India, such *Amritdhari* or *Khalsa* ('pure') Sikhs seem to be in a minority—they regard themselves as a 'leavening' in the community, the guardians of its traditions and standards. Certainly, in Britain the *Amrit* ceremony is seldom performed; I do not think it has ever been administered in Huddersfield, and it is only rarely performed in the larger *Gurdwaras*; one might expect any revival of enthusiasm for the religion to be accompanied by 'mass baptisms'; this has happened at Southall and Wolverhampton, coinciding with disputes with employers over the wearing of turbans. It seems, actually, that many of the Sikhs from simpler farming families have little idea of the meaning or even of the existence of *Khande di Pahal*.[1]

For these people, the feature that distinguishes the *pakka* Sikh from the *pattit* ('fallen') is not the *Pahal*, but the wearing of the well-known Five Symbols, and, of course, *Kesh* (long hair) is the most conspicuous and the one to which they attach most importance. In the Punjabi villages, nearly all *Jats* are *Keshdhari*, with their hair and their beards unshaven. Boys and men keep their hair tied in a top-knot (*jura*), held in place by a small curved comb (*Kanga*, another of the Five Symbols)—men cover it with a turban (*pag*). The *pag* may be tied in various styles; there is no special significance either in the style or the colour;[2] boys generally cover their *juras* with a small 'hanky' (*rumal*).

Women in the Punjab invariably keep their hair long, and braid it in a single plait, often using artificial woollen plaits to lengthen it. Girls keep their heads uncovered, often using a light scarf (*chuni*) thrown back over either shoulder; married women keep their heads covered with a scarf (*dupatta*) or shawl (*chaddar*). Young married women are expected to keep their heads covered when strangers are present, but are not required to veil their faces (unlike strict Muslims): 'Go away, go away, foolish women who hide behind veils'—this was said by Guru Arjun when a Muslim princess

---

[1] The *Amrit* ceremony is traditionally performed at the time of *Baisakhi*, the festival commemorating Guru Gobind Singh's founding of the *Khalsa* (1699), but it can be performed at any time when there is enough demand, and important *Gurdwaras* in India (notably *Takht Keshgarh, Anandpur Saheb*, the site of the original *Baisakhi*) have regular and frequent *Pahals*. It is conducted by a *Granthi* and five *Amritdhari* Sikhs—representing the *Panch Piare* of Guru Gobind Singh; they each recite a portion of *Gurbani* while water with sweets in it is stirred with a double edged knife (*Khanda*), then it is sprinkled on the hair and eyes of the initiates, who then all drink from the steel dish (*Bata*). Finally, they are reminded of the rules and prohibitions of the *Panth*, and the ceremony ends with the usual *Ardas* and *Hukm*, and distribution of *Karah Prasad*.

[2] For smart appearance, an 'under-turban' is worn which is visible in the angle of the folds on the forehead. For comfort, a strip of cloth is sometimes tied under the beard and knotted on top of the head, with the *pag* tied over it in the day-time; many *Keshdhari* Sikhs just use this when they sleep. There are certain colours for special occasions, as with women's clothes—pink or red for weddings, white for funerals, yellow for the festival of *Basant Panchmi* (the beginning of Spring, in honour of the yellow '*Sarong*'—mustard flower). *Namdharis* wear white *pags* tied straight across their foreheads. *Nihangs* and *Akalis* wear blue, with yellow under-turbans. The Sikhs in East Africa have some distinctive styles in tying their *pags*, and wear white more commonly than Punjabis do.

and her retinue wanted to attend his *Sangat* in *purdah*.

The men who first migrated to Britain almost all shaved shortly before leaving India, or when they reached Britain. Obviously, they felt that turbans and beards gave them too conspicuous an appearance, and they knew that they might encounter difficulty in getting a job (especially one where uniforms were worn). As the numbers of Sikhs in various towns increased, with wives and families, *Gurdwaras* were founded and self-contained communities developed, the wearing of *Kesh* became more common—new arrivals did not shave, and some who had shaved felt shamed into growing their hair again. *Keshdhari* Sikhs are still in a minority in Huddersfield, even amongst regular attenders at the *Gurdwara* (some *Sahijdhari*, shaven, Sikhs wear turbans to attend the *Gurdwara*, but most use handkerchiefs or scarves to cover their heads), though they are now a substantial minority—about a third of regular attenders at the *Gurdwara*. They are mainly amongst the various 'élites' in the community—teachers, bus-drivers, shopkeepers and older heads of families. Very few immigrant Sikh women have cut their hair.

A similar trend has been noticeable with the children. At first, only sons of strict Sikhs kept long hair, but the number of *Keshdhari* Sikh boys in schools has increased, and a great many boys born in Britain have not had their hair cut. A few Sikh girls have had their hair cut, but this is rare. Moreover, some Sikh parents who have had their children's hair cut expect that, when they are old enough, they may decide to grow it; there is, of course, no compulsion on a child, or an adult who is not *Amritdhari*, to keep his hair long; it is the *Amritdhari* adult Sikh who will feel it a fall from grace to cut his hair. On the other hand, orthodox Sikhs criticize others who cut their children's hair for setting a bad example.

Having long hair obviously has its inconveniences for children. It certainly makes them look markedly different from other children; in schools where there are few Sikh children, they are likely (for a time at least) to get teased for this—something that happened when and where boys were 'dispersed' to schools away from the 'immigrant neighbourhoods'. It requires much more attention in the way of washing and dressing, and necessitates wearing a bathing cap for swimming lessons. Moreover, teenage Sikhs are likely to regard it as a symbol of conformity to communal norms which they may find oppressive. They could argue, with some justification, that more important elements in the teachings of the Gurus placed emphasis on the improvement of one's character, and condemned hypocritical adherence to 'external' observances, such as the wearing of special clothes.

But they are as likely, especially after they leave school, and probably meet with hostility and discrimination, to fall back on their families and communities and begin to assert their distinctiveness with all the enthusiasm of converts in a 'revival'. Guru Gobind Singh introduced the Five Symbols at a time of demoralization, presumably to encourage a sense of communal solidarity and boldness. Sikhs whose attempts at 'anglicization' meet with rejection—on account of skin-colour and all the subtle differences of behaviour or attitude that make them 'different' from other communities in the town—may feel as besieged and oppressed as the earlier followers of the Guru. Wearing *Kesh* would be for them a symbolic act of pride in being different, like the black peoples' assertion 'Black is beautiful'. The much-publicized dispute with the Wolverhampton Transport Committee, over the right of Sikh busmen to wear turbans, created a revival of enthusiasm for wearing *Kesh* throughout the British Sikh community.[1] Certainly in Huddersfield a number of formerly *pattit* Sikhs grew hair and beards again at this time, and took part in the demonstration march in Wolverhampton.

Less conspicuous than *Kesh* or *Kanga* are *Kacche*, the 'pants' that men and women are required to wear. These are widely used as underwear, though more orthodox types of underclothing are regarded by most Sikhs as a permissible substitute. The clothing of men and boys in all other respects conforms entirely to British styles, although some men like to change into pyjama trousers (which originated as the Punjabi *pajama*) for relaxing in their homes. Teenage boys are keen to dress in 'fashionable' clothes; there is a certain inconsistency in the standards of 'fashion' that they aspire to—partly, it is the dress of their British contemporaries (apart from 'uniforms' that associate with particular groups—skinheads, greasers, hells angels and so on), but the Hindi cinema and Indian language magazines are influential in selling the rather different fashions of the Indian urban youth, which tend to be 'smooth' and 'flashy', yet more conservative than western styles. Little girls are generally dressed in British styles, and (unlike the Pakistani Muslims) girls at secondary schools usually wear the school uniform or western costume of a regular kind. Women (and girls attending the *Gurdwara*) wear the Punjabi *kamiz* and *shalwar*. The *kamiz* is a tunic, generally brightly coloured (usually only one colour) and embroidered. *Shalwar*, loose trousers gathered at the ankles, was a Muslim garment, designed to conform to the Quranic injunction to disguise the shape of the female body as well as covering the skin; however, Sikhs are not bound by such rules— they consider that a woman should keep her legs covered, but they do not mind tight-fitting *shalwar*, and western trouser-suits or similar fashions are quite acceptable to them, at least for girls. While the women avoid jobs where they would be unable to keep

[1] See David Beetham's *Transport and Turbans*. Bibliography, section 10.

this costume (at any rate some kind of overall smock and trousers), there is seldom any objection to girls wearing nurses' uniform. On the other hand, clothing can become an issue in disputes between daughters and parents (as turbans can with sons). Cases where a girl's relationship with her parents have deteriorated to a serious degree very often involve disputes over the wearing of 'Asian' dress rather than the dress and make-up fashions of English girls.

Even *Sahijdhari* (shaven) Sikhs generally wear the *Kara*, a bracelet of steel, which is another of the Five Symbols (it was probably once worn as a protection when fighting with swords, but various symbolic interpretations are placed on the Guru's command to wear it); men wear quite thick ones, ladies more delicate thin ones. Men sometimes wear gold ones, which are often exchanged as gifts by the fathers at a wedding—however, a *Kara* should strictly be made of pure steel. Otherwise, few ornaments are worn, compared with the regalia of people in other parts of India. Girls and married women wear glass bangles, which they break when their husbands die. The bride at a wedding is laden with masses of jewellery, which forms part of her dowry—ornaments for her ears, forehead, nose and lips, arms, fingers and ankles, and newly-married women continue to wear some of this for a time, but otherwise, only small earrings, necklaces and rings are worn. Women, girls and small boys wear eye make-up, *sarma* (collyrium): it is said to protect the eyes (from flies, etc.), but types containing lead are dangerous. Western cosmetics—lipstick, scents, nail-varnish and so on—are used by women and girls to an increasing extent: they would be disapproved of in a Punjabi village.

Bangles have, unfortunately, proved a danger—the steel *Kara* cannot be worn by men operating fast-moving machines in case it catches in the works (this has happened in a Huddersfield mill, with fatal results). The women's glass bangles can also cut the wrist badly if they break in an accident.

Sikhs are supposed to carry a weapon, the *Kirpan* (a short scimitar-dagger of solid steel) being the fifth of the Five symbols. This is a problem in Britain; those who want to adhere strictly to the rules generally wear or carry a miniature *Kirpan* or *Khanda*—women sometimes wear one as a kind of charm on a necklace. Otherwise, the observance is overlooked, unless a pocket-knife is considered an adequate substitute. Very pious Sikhs do occasionally wear a real *Kirpan* (hung on the left side of the waist, by a strap over the right shoulder) when attending the *Gurdwara.*

Few Sikh families in Britain may observe all these customs very rigorously, but amongst the first generation of Sikh immigrants there are certainly enough distinctive features of behaviour for their growing children to notice, and to realize that they have been born into a community which is consciously distinct and different from other communities in the neighbourhood—the majority white, working-class community (which is itself to some extent consciously 'different' from the 'common culture' taken for granted by schools, the media, and administrators), as well as other communities that have the visibly distinguishing feature of skin colour. Even if the children abandon all these observances, or even if they go to the other extreme of fanatical devotion, their personalities will develop in ambivalence which could be a source of emotional strain and desperate unhappiness. On the other hand, if their upbringing at home and in school combines a sense of security with the growth of self-confidence, it is as likely to be a source of creativity.

5 Home

Awareness of belonging to a 'different' community, with traditions markedly unlike those of other children, will not be limited to the notice the child takes of his parents' religious observances; as we have seen, religious practices are indistinguishable from social customs, and everyday, homely matters like dress or food become important and obvious distinguishing marks of the community. It is a journalistic exaggeration to call the home life of Sikhs in Britain 'little India'—even the most conservative immigrants have made substantial changes in their ways of life under the pressure of local housing conditions, climate, hours and types of work, home furnishings, sanitary arrangements and so on; but the Sikh child does grow up in a home where life is, in certain respects, quite different from life in the homes of other children here.

'Home' in Huddersfield is, typically, in a back-to-back terraced house of late Victorian or Edwardian vintage, solidly built of stone, and generally fit for 'improvement' rather than demolition. There are a few areas of the town, limited to single streets and adjacent terraces, which are occupied entirely by immigrant families, but in no case are they exclusively in the hands of one community, and in these 'immigrant' neighbourhoods there are numbers of 'white' immigrant families—from Europe and Ireland—and so there are no 'all coloured' areas. Most Sikh families live in 'mixed' areas, where the population has remained fairly stable over four or five years, after the initial 'panic' when the first immigrants bought houses in these areas. From the outside, there is seldom much to distinguish a Sikh house from any other, but Indian tastes in exterior decoration are noticeable in some cases, with the woodwork painted in bright pastel shades and the stonework around the doors and windows also painted in vivid colours; such ornamentation provoked comment, it was certainly conspicuous in streets of uniformly grimy stone houses. In the last few years, there has been less colourful painting done, and attempts are made to conform to the local customs—several Sikh families have had their house fronts sandblasted or stonepainted. Standards in maintaining the houses in good repair vary, but most are proud of their houses and many are keen handymen; there is certainly no sign that these immigrants are less careful than their neighbours in looking after their houses, and the fathers train their sons to help them with work on the house.

In furnishing their homes, the Sikhs have apparently adapted very much to British styles. Like respectable working-class families, they furnish the 'front room' of the terrace house with a three piece suite, television and coffee-table, and use it for entertaining guests. Kitchen and bedroom furnishings are still sometimes relatively sparse—lacking many cupboards, drawers, or dressers. Telephones, refrigerators, vacuum cleaners, and all the paraphernalia of western domesticity are common; but still there is a certain 'Indian' character to it: the television covered when not in use with an embroidered cloth, the pictures of the Gurus or of family elders decorated with tinsels; even fairy lights over the mantelpiece. Perhaps the 'model' is the home of the urban middle-class family in India (as idealized by the advertisements in Indian newspapers and as portrayed in the Hindi films) rather than a purely 'western' home.

One feature of home life that the Punjabis have not changed to any great degree is their food; the meals a Sikh child takes at home are very different from the dinners he may have at school, and basically resemble, as closely as mother can manage, the food eaten by *Jats* in the Punjabi villages. What one may or may not eat is a matter of intense concern to Indians—witness the sporadic riots over cow-slaughter—and it is an important feature of *Dharam*, but the Sikhs are rather less hedged about by regulations in this respect than are the Hindus or Muslims. Sophisticated Sikhs would sum up the Guru's teaching as an instruction to eat whatever is good for you (except for food offered to idols and *halal* meat, which we shall discuss later). As we have mentioned, they attach great importance to the *Guru ka Langar*, where food is prepared and eaten by people irrespective of caste or any of the other factors which divide Hindu communities.[1]

The main elements in the diet of Punjabis both in India and in Britain are cereal products, fresh vegetables, milk products, pulses, sugar products and fruit. Gas is favoured for Punjabi-style cookery as a naked flame is necessary. Most cooking is done on top of the cooker—simmering, frying and griddling; the grill is used for browning *chapattis* and puffing them up; the oven is seldom used, except as a warming cupboard. Some ladies did not like standing up to cook, being used to sitting or squatting in front of a *chuli* (a small clay oven with an open fire in it) in India. The main cooking utensils are a range of saucepans, an iron griddle (*tawa*)—either flat of slightly concave, with a long handle. Pressure

---

[1] There are fanatical *Akalis* and *Nihangs* who would not eat food prepared by anyone who is not a member of their *Jatha*, and would not eat after—say— shaking hands with an outsider until they had washed and ritually purified themselves. I met (and shook hands!) with such 'pure' Sikhs in India, but doubt if there are any such in Britain.

cookers are widely used, for steaming operations that would otherwise take several hours. Flour and spices are usually bought from Asian grocers ready ground, but some women have a pestle and mortar for crushing spices. Food is served in bowls, with side dishes (fresh vegetables, pickles, curds and so on) on side plates. It is necessary to have *chapattis* freshly cooked so mother and daughters will go on making these while the men in the family are eating; otherwise they are kept warm by wrapping in a towel. Food is eaten with the fingers, pieces of *chapattis* being used to pick up and hold pieces of food, and also as 'spoons' to pick up liquids; spoons are used quite a lot, but not knives or forks.

Punjabis are accustomed to taking a good meal in the morning and evening. Breakfast is often somewhat anglicized—corn flakes, eggs, and tea are as common as any other menus, and sliced bread is found more convenient in the morning than *chapattis*; but many families prefer the traditional Punjabi breakfast of *paraunthas* (see below) stuffed with vegetable and eaten with curds, accompanied by milk, buttermilk or tea. The main meal is taken in the evening, just before going to bed.

Food of any kind in colloquial Punjabi is *roti* (bread), and unleavened bread forms the backbone of the diet. It is made from wheat flour (*kanak da atta*).[1] The basic form of *roti* is the familiar *chapatti*, a pancake of flour and water with a little salt, well kneaded and patted or rolled out flat; it is cooked on an iron griddle (*tawa*) —as it cooks, it swells up and should be pressed down with a cloth; it can be finished off under a hot grill or in a naked flame. A *parauntha* (Hindi *paratha*) is made in the same way, but butter is incorporated in the dough; vegetables are sometimes stuffed between two *paraunthe*, which are then pressed together and cooked. A *puri* is made with finer-ground wheat-flour, and is deep-fried in clarified butter.

Vegetables are eaten daily, generally bought from Asian shops, from the market or town supermarkets; however, many Sikhs have taken to growing vegetables in their gardens (most terraced houses in this town have garden plots, albeit small; a few Punjabis have rented allotments from the Corporation, reviving a local occupation that was dying out). The most typical Punjabi food is *sag*, made from mustard leaves (*sarong*) chopped, finely flavoured with salt and aromatics (mainly ground ginger), and eaten with generous amounts of butter. Mustard, of course, grows in Britain, but the leaves are not lush enough here to make good *sag*. Imported tinned leaves are not liked, because they are of poor quality and the stalks are not trimmed off, spoiling the flavour. A popular substitute is

[1] In Punjabi villages, maize or millet flour (*maki, bajre da atta*) is quite often preferred, and maize flour is sold in Asian shops here but is less widely used; it makes *roti* that is bright yellow, tastier but more brittle and less easy to digest than that made of wheat flour, and traditionally accompanies *sarong da sag* (mustard leaves).

made from spinach (*palak*) and spring greens (*band-gobi*), separately or mixed together, or else mixed with tinned or home-grown *sarong*. The Punjabi diet includes many vegetables that are grown in temperate climates and so are readily available in Britain, and can be grown in gardens—cauliflower (*gobi*), potatoes (*alu*), peas (*mattar*), carrots (*gajar*), Jerusalem artichokes (*arvi*), turnips (*shalgam*), tomatoes (*tamatar*) and so on. A few that are not indigenous have nevertheless been grown here with some success by Sikh gardeners—long radishes (*muli*), fenugreek (*metha*) for example. Other vegetables that were favourites in the Punjab are less easily available here, and have to be in the 'special treat' category: aubergines (*bataon*) and okra (*bhindi*) are sold by Asian shops, but are expensive; *tindas* and *karelas* (bitter melons) are only available in tins.

Milk products are a major source of protein and fat in the Punjabi diet. Butter (*makhan*) is eaten in large quantities, not only on unleavened bread, but mixed with vegetables and other cooked foods. Clarified butter (*ghee*) is the main cooking fat—it is quite good for frying as it does not burn easily, but it is expensive in Britain to buy butter in sufficient quantities for these purposes, and some families have taken to using vegetable oils (which will probably be better for them!). Curds (*dehi*), sometimes salted or spiced, at other times sweetened, accompany most meals; these are generally home-cured, but 'natural' yogurt sold in local shops is used (commercially sweetened and flavoured yogurt is not liked, understandably). Buttermilk (*lassi*) was the traditional morning drink of Punjabis, at least until tea became popular there, but it is not easy to obtain here, and commercially produced buttermilk is not as tasty as that made in the villages from buffalo milk. A fatty kind of cottage cheese (*panir*) is made at home; it is firm enough in consistency to stew or fry without breaking up, and is eaten cooked, or mixed with a cooked dish.

Pulses (*dal*) form a valuable source of protein in the diet; they sound uninteresting food, but in fact there are a great many varieties (Asian shops here stock at least ten or twelve—*masrani* lentils, *channa* chick-peas, *mung* small green beans, *urad* black beans, and so on), which may be whole or split, and they can be lightly cooked and kept solid, or stewed to a purée; flavourings can be cooked with the *dal*, or added afterwards, so that great variety is possible.

Sikhs are thought of by vegetarian Hindus as meat-eaters, but this is rather misleading. Many Sikhs are vegetarians, notably the members of sects such as the *Radhasoami Satsang*, the *Namdharis* and the *Udasis*, and this is true of a substantial minority of Sikhs in Britain. They are all forbidden (by Guru Gobind Singh) to eat meat that has been offered to idols, or the *Halal* (Kosher) meat of Muslims, though Sikh shopkeepers don't mind selling it to Pakistani customers; in practice, they are unlikely to be offered meat in either category. On the other hand, they are likely to be offered beef, for example with school dinners; beef is not eaten in the Punjab, because the Hindus feel so strongly about killing the sacred cow, and most Sikhs believe that they are forbidden to kill cattle or eat beef, though the intellectuals amongst them would say that this is only due to Hindu influence. The majority of Sikhs who do eat meat do so on special occasions—festivals, weddings, or entertaining visitors—and in Britain more often, once a week or more. Chicken is the favourite, skinned, rubbed with aromatics and fricasséed. Lamb and mutton are also liked—replacing goat which is popular in the Punjab. Pork, other types of fowl, bird and animal game, and fish are less commonly eaten, though they are liked as a change. A few English meat and fish dishes have become quite popular in Sikh homes, especially with the children who eat them at school or with friends—fish and chips is the most common, and fish fingers, sausages and canned fish (like tuna) are liked. Eggs are eaten (but not by *Radhasoami Satsangis*, who regard them as meat) usually hard-boiled or as omelettes.

Punjabi food is of course 'spicier' than English, and English food served as school dinners must taste rather dull by comparison. Punjabi food does not, however, consist of 'curry' as generally imagined, still less of rice, and is mildly flavoured by comparison with the real curries of South India and Bengal. The basic aromatics in most dishes are onions (*piaz*), garlic (*lassang*), salt (*lung*) and peppers (*mirch*), these being black peppers (*kala mirch* or *chota mirch*) and green or red chillis, either whole, ground whole, or just the seeds ground. Other spices commonly used are turmeric (*haldi*), ginger (*adrak*—if ground, it is *sont*), cummin seeds (*jira*), coriander (*dhannia*—the seeds and the leaves are used; it is one of the few spices used in the Punjab that can be grown here), cardamoms (*ilachi*—small green ones are chewed after meals, as well as being used, like the bigger brown ones, in cooking), fenugreek leaves and seeds (*methi*) and mustard seeds (*rai*). These are all sold in Asian shops, by the pound, and are surprisingly cheap when compared with spices sold in English shops in one ounce packets.

Special occasions are marked by avoiding *roti* and other things made of flour; instead, rice is eaten, in the form of a *pilao* (generally eaten separately—rice is not usually mixed with meat or vegetable dishes, as it is in the Central Indian or Bengali cookery practised in Indian restaurants) or *kher*, a superior rice pudding. Other sweet dishes include various types of halwa, including *karah* (the semolina sweet served as *Prashad* in *Gurdwaras*), and *gajarella* or *gajar pak* (made of carrots and dried milk). There are many confections sold by Asian shops here, including Pakistani *halwai* (sweet shops)—*jalebis*, *burfi*, *ladu*, *gulab jaman*, and *rashgullas*; these are difficult to make at home, but a Bombay firm is exporting 'instant mixes' to Britain for some of the things, and they are quite successful. English sweets and sweet dishes are well liked, especially by the children—tinned fruits, rice pudding, and, of course, ice-cream; these replace raw sugar-cane and sugar-sweets loved by children in the Punjab.

Various savouries as snack dishes are becoming quite familiar here—*samosas* and *pakauras*, made with vegetables in batter are often served to visitors and at parties. 'Curry' (*khari* in Punjabi) is a kind of soup made of gram flour (*besan*). Pickles (*acchar*) are generally eaten with meals—of lime, mango, chillis, lotus or water-lily root and other things, also chutney (*chatni*, a simple form of *chat*, which is a 'sweet and sour' dish made with vegetables and fruit).

Tea is the favourite beverage; water is boiled, then tea and generous amounts of milk and sugar are added, and the mixture warmed again; sometimes aniseed (*sonf*) and, occasionally, salt are added.[1]

The Punjabis consider this a very healthy diet, and they certainly keep fit on it; being a very mixed race, they vary a good deal in appearance, but tend (unlike people from other parts of India) to be as tall and heavy as British people, and some are strikingly tall. The children are chubby and strong. In the Punjab, many live to a good old age, and remain very fit to the end, probably on account of a good diet and hard-working but relatively unhurried way of life. There seems little support for the belief that Sikh children in England are undernourished or prone to disease. Their parents are willing to make use of public medical services and to take the advice of doctors and nurses. There remains a certain amount of belief in herbal and homeopathic medicines as preventatives and cures for minor ailments. Tropical diseases—typhoid, cholera, smallpox, polio, leprosy, malaria and so on—have *not* been 'imported' by Sikh immigrants. Even tuberculosis, which has been rather common amongst immigrants from certain areas in Pakistan, is rare amongst the Sikh immigrants.

Sikhs are very careful about personal hygiene—we have mentioned the importance attached to cleanliness in connection with religion. They wash themselves all over daily, and bathe and wash their hair frequently, as is necessary in view of its length and the type of work they do; they wash their hands before eating. Early immigrants were unfamiliar with pedestal-type toilets, and preferred washing with water to using toilet-paper, but there has been widespread adaption in these respects. They are accustomed to cleaning their teeth daily, but the children's teeth are as subject as those of other children to the ravages of sweets. However, they do not smoke, and this keeps their teeth whiter.

Guru Gobind Singh's ban on smoking is very generally observed;

[1] This is a new habit in the Punjab; an older generation of Sikhs was very suspicious of tea, and drank only buttermilk.

it is very rare to find a Sikh who smokes. On the other hand, a great many of the men do drink. It is the opposite with the Muslims and Hindus—they smoke a lot, but most do not drink. In fact, the Guru did, on several occasions, forbid drinking amongst his Sikhs, but this command is largely overlooked; a possible reason why the ban on drinking is neglected while that on smoking is strictly observed is that the latter is a distinctive feature of the Sikh religion, marking off the Sikhs from Muslims and Hindus. On the other hand, the Sikhs' reputation for drunkenness is not really deserved—there are many Sikh teetotallers, and more who only drink in moderation. The men have taken very readily to English beer-drinking habits, though the custom of buying 'rounds' in turn cuts across their idea of the roles of 'host' and 'guest'; they have also taken up such ancillary pastimes as darts, dominoes, and the one-arm bandit. Drink in the Punjab is mainly spirits, home-made from raw sugar (*desi sharab*); spirits are liked by Sikh men in Britain, especially whisky and rum, which are the nearest in taste to *desi sharab*, and are consumed very freely at weddings and other parties; Pernod, the liqueur 'anis' closely resembling Punjabi *sonfia* distilled from aniseed (*sonf*), is also liked, but regarded as excessively expensive.

We must complete our picture of the home life of Sikh children in Britain by returning to some of the points we considered in the chapter on 'Childhood'. The home life of the older Sikh child, of school age, is a natural development of the patterns established in infancy. Time is passed playing with other children, as we have described, helping mother or father, dressing, eating, sleeping, going shopping, visiting relatives and so on. For the child, a most important element in all this is imaginative. His developing imagination feeds on stories, whether told by mother or teacher, seen on television or at the cinema or read in comics, on imitative play, on ritual—in religious observances and in games—and on songs and music. In the 'folk-psychology' of India, the period of childhood from the coming of second teeth up to puberty (the period known as *kumara*) is regarded as one in which imagination and feeling dominates reason. Parents expect imaginative, dramatic play to replace the simply imitative play mentioned in an account of infancy; they expect children of this age to love stories, music and all that appeals to the feelings and sense of excitement—the colour and sounds of a wedding, sweets at *Diwali* and *Lohri*, the the saturnalian freedom of *Holi*, squirting coloured water. In Britain, these are, as we have mentioned, replaced by the local festivals that punctuate a child's life—Christmas, birthdays, summer outings—and by relatively 'passive' entertainment, the television and cinema. To a considerable extent, the Sikh child shares the common imaginative culture of other children here, as purveyed by television, by comics and by the efforts of teachers, but there are certain elements in most British children's imaginative repertoire that Sikh children cannot be assumed to know—particularly the 'nursery' stories and rhymes that are generally learnt before entry to nursery or infants school. On the other hand, they are heirs to a rich and flourishing culture, which is, to a certain extent, being passed on to them by their parents and older brothers and sisters.

Story-telling is traditional in the Punjab, and there is a variety of amusing or exciting stories which are told to children by their grandmothers and other older relatives; in Britain, the older relatives are not present, and not all mothers and fathers have the time, knowledge or inclination to relate stories to their children, who then get all their imaginative stimulus from television. But this is not always the case, and it is likely that Sikh children will have knowledge of a range of stories which their schoolteachers could well draw on if they want to give these children an opportunity to make a positive contribution to the work of a multi-racial school.

The most widely known stories are about the Gurus, especially Guru Nanak; they are legends, similar to the miracle stories in the Bible and the European saints' legends, that were attached to the biographies of these teachers by popular imagination, and were incorporated in the *Janam Sakhis* (legendaries) of Guru Nanak, and *Sakhis* of other Gurus, from where they passed back, through the teachings of *Gianis* in the *Gurdwaras*, into oral tradition. They are something of an embarrassment to sophisticated Sikhs, who feel, with justification, that they give a very false impression of the lives and teachings of the Gurus—who all condemned miracle-workers and popular superstition. The stories that make up the *Sakhis* can be divided into three categories: there are anecdotes that are certainly historical, being evidenced in non-Sikh sources—in the lives of the later Gurus, from Guru Arjun onwards, there are many such incidents, for the Sikhs had become a force to be reckoned with by the Mughal emperors and so are frequently mentioned by the court historians; then there are stories which, though not capable of historical proof, are credible, free of miracles and crude superstition, and illustrating some moral point in the Guru's teaching—for example, the story of the three sons of Guru Ram Das, and how the youngest proved his loyalty; finally, there are the crude folkstories, in which the Gurus contend with witches and giants, using magic to defeat them. The Sikh Missionary Society has done useful work in circulating good English versions of stories in the first two categories, but the stories told in *Gurdwaras*, and passed on by pious parents to their children are not so critically selected.

There are also some secular stories, mostly romances, the finest of which have the universal quality of classic tragedy; these, again, probably originated as folk-stories, but were in some cases clothed in literary form and then returned to oral tradition. The one generally regarded as the greatest is *Heer Ranjha*, of which there are at least three literary versions, but the earliest and best loved is by Warris Shah—it has a 'Romeo and Juliet' theme of lovers whose families are at war; films have been made of it, but of poor quality. *Sassi Pannu* similarly ends with lovers separated by their parents united in the grave; *Sohni Mahiwal* is a story of an unhappily married girl who swims every night to visit her lover across the river, and finally they drown in each other's arms; *Mirza Sahiban* has been mentioned as an example of the popular Punjabi theme, a girl who places love for her brothers above devotion to her lover, though they do not return her love. These stories, typically of star-crossed lovers, whose parents will not let them marry, tyrannous mothers-in-law and elopements, reveal the tensions and conflicting loyalties that can exist in the extended family.[1]

There are other stories that have not, so far as I know, been given literary form, but are on similar archetypal themes. They tend to be more rambling, with less concentration on psychological issues than the 'classics'—the story of the King who asked his three daughters, like King Lear, whom they loved best in all the world, the story of Rup and Basant, two brothers (like Lord Rama and Lakshman) exiled by a jealous stepmother, or the story of *Dhruv* (the Pole Star) in which another jealous stepmother appears. Others are more in the nature of 'genre' anecdotes and fables—the foolish boy robber who disturbs the people he is trying to rob, the fisherman who caught a golden fish, and the woodman who managed to stretch a single lucky wish to cover all he wanted in life. There are also semi-historical stories, such as those of Kikkar Singh, a wrestler of the last century who got his name by tearing up acacia trees, and the stories that have accumulated around the life of Bhagat Singh, a Punjabi freedom fighter executed by the British in 1932, who has become something of a 'Robin Hood' figure, and is portrayed on many calendars and posters; films have been made of his life.

These stories—some of them, at least—will form part of the child's fantasy alongside stories from English tradition heard at school, and the modern folk-lore of spies and spacemen purveyed by television and comics which they devour avidly. There is another source of imaginary material which is not accessible to other children, the Indian cinema; an Indian film society has held weekly shows for nearly ten years, and other Asian films societies have existed from time to time. They show the products of the flourishing film industry in India—massive epics of escapism, lasting three hours at least, and sometimes five, filled with battle, murder, sudden death, incredible coincidences and appalling sentimentality. While they derive their technique from the great days of Hollywood, their

---

[1] The great Persian romance *Laila Majnun* (immortalized by Nizami), another story of star-crossed lovers, is also found in the repertoire of Punjabi stories.

subject matter, the social conventions that underlie their stories, and the conventions of fantasy that have to be accepted by the audience are entirely Indian. Already, children accustomed to the relative slickness of the television thriller say they find these films too slow, too far-fetched, and the physical, social and imaginative setting of these films can only be partly intelligible to children brought up in Britain.

Television is certainly important in these children's lives. It is watched, regularly, with absorption—bed-time is not strictly enforced in many Sikh households; younger children are trusted to go to bed when they are tired, or they fall asleep in an armchair, and older children go to bed when their parents do (but they get into trouble if they stay out late with friends). The Sunday morning television programme in Hindi is watched in most families, and is a source of 'information about life in Britain'—as the BBC put it—as well as another source of Indian-style entertainment by singers, comedians and visiting film-stars; it suffers by comparison with other television programmes from rather amateurish presentation. The same applies to the radio programme that precedes it, which is mainly a record request programme, with a few interviews and chatty interludes.

The music played on these programmes, and on the overseas services of All India Radio and Radio Pakistan (which families with short-wave radios listen to), and recorded on tape by many fathers or elder brothers, is mainly film-music, sung by 'playback singers'; the actors in Indian films mime and dance to these songs. The phrasing, tonality and, to some extent, rhythm of these songs is Indian, but the orchestration western, with incongruous mixtures of Mantovani-like string and piano effects and Indian instruments; between East and West, they fall into a fairly uniform schmaltziness, relieved only when a composer attempts to recapture the spirit of indigenous folk-music.

Punjabi music is quite different from this, and is occasionally heard on the radio programmes; there are professional folk singers and dancers who make profitable tours of Punjabi settlements in Britain, and it is a music which is preserved and revived by amateurs within the community. It is technically based on modal and rhythmic patterns (*ragas* and *talas*) like the *Sangit* of Hindu India, but it shows strong influences from successive waves of invaders who have crossed through the Punjab—from Iran and the Middle East, and from Afghanistan and the south of the U.S.S.R. Unlike Indian classical music, it is vigorous and direct, with flowing rhythms matching dramatic lyrics. It is a vehicle for the uninhibited expression of joy or grief.

The most characteristic examples are the rhythmic songs that accompany the folk-dance—*Bhangra* and *Gidha*. These were originally harvest rituals, but are now performed whenever there is any possible excuse for rejoicing. The rhythm of *Bhangra*, the men's dance, is generally provided by one or more large side drums played with sticks (*dholak*—the tones of the two ends of the drum differ as treble and bass), but in *Gidha*, the girls' dance, clapping replaces the drumming. The dancers in either case form two rows, or a circle or half-circle; in the centre, pairs of dancers sing and gesture dramatically, 'leading' the dance—thus the dance-song is antiphonal, one of the 'leaders' singing a solo line, to which the chorus respond as they dance round; the 'leaders' change after each 'verse'. While the rhythm of the chorus and the general form of the dance is fixed, there is no limit to improvisation in the lyrics, gestures and steps. The classic *Bhangra* song is about sowing and harvesting, with the actions mimed, the *Gidha* is the women's call, 'Wake up, farmer, the corn is ripe!' There are also traditional lyrics for festivals, seasons of the year and family occasions—births and weddings—but singers are expected to make up topical words to suit the occasion; sometimes, lyrics are made up on the spot, commenting on the audience or the event, and there are songs that are pure expressions of joy in living and the beauty of the Punjabi countryside that must create nostalgia in the minds of migrants. Similarly, the traditional skipping step of the dance is varied with leaps and acrobatic feats like Cossack dancing. *Bhangra* dancers wear brightly-coloured cloths wrapped round their waists and flapping over both legs (*chadra, lahnga*) and embroidered waistcoats; they have straps of bells on their ankles and streamers on their wrists, and the ends of their turbans flap loose. *Gidha* dancers sometimes wear skirts (*lungi*), pleated and flared, instead of *shalwar*, and arrange their scarves in little peaks, looking very colourful. There are a few other dances, such as *Tipri*, in which girls carry short sticks which they tap with each other for the rhythm—there is no singing with this dance. Some older Sikh girls, who learnt these dances in the Punjab, incorporate them in their play.

One can only hint at the wide range of subject-matter, senti-ment and style of the folk-songs. There are songs for all occasions —birth, lullabies, the landmarks of childhood, songs for all stages in wedding celebrations, and elegies for the dead. The songs that relate and expand episodes in the great classical stories are amongst the most magnificent—especially loved is *Doli charhdian mariyan Heer chikan*, the song of Heer when she is forcibly married to a man she hates. Some songs tell a complete story, like a ballad— in one, a boy leaves his child-bride to go to war; when he returns, he does not recognize the beautiful woman who is his wife. There are humorous ballads, like the story of a simple woman whose husband was rewarded for bravery by being made an officer, and the glory goes to her head when she leaves her mud hut to live in a bungalow. Sad themes feature in the songs of soldiers longing for their homes, songs of girls whose brothers are at war (a characteristic Punjabi theme); different tensions within the family structure are expressed in songs of girls wishing a husband would take them away from drudgery at home, and of married women wishing they were back with their parents. Love songs, highly stylized or simple and direct, are popular, especially the couplets known as *tappe*. These are living genres of folk-song, and people still compose in them, but many are still popular in spite of great antiquity; a great favourite dates from the eighteenth-century depredations of Nadir Shah, in which a Hindu girl tells how she was rescued from her kidnappers after her father had been killed, her brother had run away and her husband had disowned her 'by wild-looking men on lean horses carrying rusty weapons, who called themselves lions (Singhs)'.

Songs such as these are known to many Sikh parents here, and are sung at weddings and festivals, but there is little inclination to pass on this tradition. The more sophisticated Sikhs think, unfortunately, that these things are the amusements of 'uneducated' and 'rustic' (*desi*) people, while the more pious are only interested in maintaining belief in religion, not in 'secular' songs and stories. The music in the *Gurdwaras* is to some extent part of the folk-tradition, though it is more obviously bound by the traditional forms of the *ragas* in which the contents of the *Guru Granth Saheb* are composed and by which they are classified. The same percussion instruments form the 'backbone' of religious and secular music—drums (*tabla*) and side-drums (*dholi, dhola* and *dholak*—the smaller *dholi* and *dhola* are played with the palms of the hands). Melody in the religious music is generally provided by a small box-type harmonium, which has regrettably superseded other, more musical instruments; there are, however, a number of Sikhs in the town who can play the traditional stringed instruments and pipes; the *sarangi*, a fiddle played with a convex bow and stopped with the finger nails, which produces a shrill, haunting sound with a 'drone' on 'sympathetic' strings; the *thumba* and *thumbi*, smaller one-stringed instruments, held horizontally and plucked, or bowed like a *sarangi*; the *bansri*, a simple flute, and *langoja*, a pair of end-blown 'Pan-pipes' played simultaneously. These are occasionally used to accompany religious music, and are brought out on joyful occasions. One hopes that at least a few Sikh children will learn to play them.

Apart from the religious music at the *Gurdwara*, the visits of professional concert-parties, and the celebrations at birth and wedding-parties, there are chances for Sikh children to hear Punjabi folk-songs, and sometimes see dances, at the festivals organized by the Indian Workers' Association to celebrate Independence Day (15 August) and Republic Day (26 January). On these occasions, the inevitable political speeches are interspersed with performance of songs and sometimes dances by members of the community; such occasions are well attended, mainly because such entertainment is enjoyed—purely political meetings attract much smaller audiences, but these are family occasions supported by everyone who can come. They are an important expression of communal self-awareness, and, as time goes on, it will be interesting to see how great an interest the young generation of British Sikhs will take in these affairs—the initial, nationalistic motive might seem meaningless to them, but a desire to identify with the community and to maintain its traditions might still motivate them. The culture of the Punjab finds expression in music and dance, stories and handicrafts as much as in the more 'intellectual' forms of novels, poetry and painting—though there has been an important 'revival' in all these spheres in India, and there are writers and artists of merit amongst 'first generation' Punjabis in Britain. There is a possibility that, as happened in India, anglicized Punjabis will affect to despise *desi* culture, preferring to teach their children English nursery rhymes and suchlike. Teenagers, not surprisingly, show interest in Western pop music, films and so on. Parents fear this to some extent, as a sign of rebelliousness and rejection of traditions, but this is usually a rather superficial adoption of 'fashions'. There is at present no dearth of Punjabi writers, singers, orators, and poets amongst the Sikhs in Britain. The inherent political-mindedness of the Sikhs is fed by numerous newspapers and magazines representing political and religious factions amongst Sikhs in various British towns—Southall, Gravesend and the West Midlands—which provide vehicles for writers of essays and short-stories as well as amateur journalists. Poems and songs are composed (often by people with little education or knowledge of the written language) for special occasions like weddings, Independence Day and so on. Political satire is also a popular subject for verse—an Indian Workers' Association meeting a day after one of Mr. Powell's outbursts was enlivened by a number of speakers who had composed attacks on racialism in Punjabi verse, and the celebrations of Guru Nanak's quincentenary were greatly prolonged to allow all the poets who had composed verses for the occasion a chance to recite them.

I am in no position to judge the quality of these effusions, but there is no doubt that Sikh children are living in an environment in which the Punjabi language—like Punjabi dress, food, music, and stories, and the Sikh religion—is an important vehicle for self-expression and communal cohesion. In our next chapter we must consider further its role in their lives.

6 Language and Education

Much of what has been said or written about children of immigrants has identified them as a 'problem' to teachers and schools. It is unfortunate that statistics are collected of children of immigrants that do not distinguish between the frightened new arrival from overseas and the child who has spent most of or all his life in Britain, between the child who cannot speak a word of English and requires full-time specialist teaching and the star pupil in a grammar school. All are lumped together and labelled 'problems'. Amongst the children born locally to immigrant parents, there is a wider range of ability than teachers in nursery and infant reception classes have ever encountered—between the child whose knowledge of English and understanding of the 'English' environment is hardly better than that of a child newly-arrived from India, to the child who is obviously very much 'at home', apparently able to manage very well in English. What is more, the whole pre-school experience of these children, which we have tried to describe in some detail, is in many ways different from that of the other children in the school; the teacher cannot take much for granted with these children. In this sense, then, they are a 'problem'. Their presence challenges the known and tried techniques of experienced teachers—they represent a range of different backgrounds, and they have difficulties—with language and with understanding the environment—which require careful attention. They cannot all be taught as if they were an identical type of child.

Teachers find that Sikh children are, in general, well-motivated and they show a genuine enthusiasm for all that is done in the classroom which is very pleasing, bearing in mind especially the possible shock-effect of coming into an environment so different from home—the unfamiliar language, the unfamiliar ways of behaviour, towards adults and other children, and the strangeness of the noise, activity and richness of things that a child experiences in a good nursery or infants classroom. Sikh parents certainly have an enthusiasm for education with which their children are inculcated; the first generation of male immigrants are mostly literate in Punjabi—those educated before 1947 in Urdu, and a few in Hindi—though there are some who never went to school;

amongst the women, too, there are relatively few who had no education. However, education has not been universally available in the Punjab until the present generation.

Education is seen mainly as a way of acquiring social standing: in India, it is a way of breaking out of the rigidity of the caste system. The *Granthi* in the traditional Punjabi village was highly respected, as the man who could communicate the words of the Guru (*Gurbani*), interpreting the symbols on the pages of the *Guru Granth Saheb*; children were introduced to him in a ceremony designed to inculcate reverence for the teacher. But learning was limited to reading and reciting from the *Guru Granth*. In the schools established by governments, British and Independent, too, a simple view of education was encouraged—a kind of ritual, which involved memorizing a great deal of information, largely out of any meaningful context, in order to pass examinations and, when enough of these were passed, to obtain 'qualifications'.

Of course, much of what we understand by the term 'education' is assumed by Sikh parents to take place at home. It is there, as we have described, that the child learns to interpret his environment, it is there that he acquires practical skills in order to master it, and it is there that he is trained to live in human society. The norms—morality, good manners, religious belief, politics, even the choice of job and marriage partner—are taken for granted, as essential functions of the life of the family and the community. The idea that these matters should be the objects of questioning and comparison with other possibilities would, of course, be as disruptive and revolutionary in a stable, tradition-bound peasant community as it is inevitable in a complex, changing industrial society. Sikh parents do not expect schools to have much to do in these respects, except to reinforce what is taken for granted.

Two of the most important elements in nursery and infant education are 'play' and the active use of language—both being necessary for a child to come to terms with his physical and social environment. Indian parents regard these as things to be done at home; the school is firstly a place where a child learns to read. A child in school is expected to be 'serious'. As he grows older, he is expected to devote more and more time and energy to 'study', that is, preparation for examinations. Enthusiastic parents will buy books for their children, but they are likely to look for text-books and digests for 'cramming'; the first-generation immigrant who reads for pleasure is something of a rarity. Teenagers are expected to be at home in the evenings, studying, or attending classes; if they stay out late with friends, this is frowned upon. Some parents employ private tutors.

This kind of motivation can, of course, create problems. Some parents, who came to Britain with high ambitions for themselves and met with frustration, transfer these ambitions to their children

—'All I care about now is my children; I shall make as much money as I can to let them have a good education.' This places a terrible burden on the children to fulfil these ambitions. This attitude to education fosters extreme competitiveness and anxiety. The children's anxiety is only increased by the fact that British schools, especially at Infant and Junior level, are not exclusively geared to this kind of exam-orientated work; 'play' is seen by parents as the opposite of 'work', and therefore not an educational activity, and parents often doubt the value even of organized games. Again, success in school depends on many things besides ability in rote-learning, notably skills with language. If a child works very hard trying to 'learn' what he does not really understand, and finds that he is still failing to achieve his parents' ambitions for him, anxiety and frustration can reach a dangerous level. A few parents, believing that their children 'are not learning anything' remove them to private schools or to private boarding schools in India. The Dagshai public school at Simla, and various Sikh schools in Delhi cater very largely for children of expatriate Sikhs. Yet, as we have seen, the traditional ways of bringing up young children do, to some extent, encourage initiative, inquisitiveness and the urge to explore, and Sikhs with relatively little formal education have proved themselves capable of adapting to the requirements of a society very different from their own, and to jobs requiring skills which they never learnt at home or at school.

The first thing the teacher needs is an understanding of the child's home life—the life of the family and the community. Sikh parents with their enthusiasm for the education of their children are pleased if they feel that their child is in the hands of a teacher who is interested in him as an individual, and are appreciative when they see the results of good teaching, especially as the child gains in understanding and confidence in the use of English. They expect their child to be taught systematically, and this is fair enough—even the superficially fluent bilingual child is likely to need training in the construction of good English sentences, especially the more complex kinds, and in the expansion of his vocabulary. Systematic teaching is not incompatible with freedom of choice and expression—it is necessary to give the children the means of expression and the understanding they need to make choices. Contact with parents is most important, preferably, in the first instance, in the home—the traditional 'open night' or parents' association does not achieve contact between the teacher and the parents he most needs to talk to. Language can, of course, be an obstacle, and teachers who deal with many children of Punjabi-speaking parents are likely to need to learn the language, though a lot can be achieved by simply being present in a child's home, exchanging the most casual pleasantries with the child himself as interpreter. The teacher, at least, is learning, and a bridgehead is established between the two worlds.

We have described some of the ways in which the life of a Sikh family in Britain is distinctly different from the life of members of any other class or community in this country—the structure of the family, religious beliefs and observances, clothes, food and entertainment. The Sikh child grows up to become more and more aware of the distinctiveness of such features—but the most important aspect of the ambivalent environment in which he develops is language, the fact that these children, whether they are dull or brilliant, have in the first few years of their lives to master two completely different languages, that is to say, two different series of interpretations and conceptualizations of the human environment, and two different codes for surviving and managing in the social environment.

We mentioned in considering the life of these children as babies, how their mothers teach them 'baby talk', how they encourage them to explore round about them, how they are the objects of attention from adults and older brothers and sisters—all this is very valuable for them. As they explore their homes and nearby, and are taken shopping or out on visits to relatives, to the park, the *Gurdwara* and so on, they begin to make sense of the succession of images, feelings and memories as their elders teach them to name things, say things about what they observe, and ask for what they want. It is only through language that anything but the most rudimentary kind of consciousness can develop. The ability of children to understand and learn in school must depend very largely on the kind of language-training and experience they had as babies. Moreover, it is the means whereby the child comes to communicate with other people, and so to understand and to function in society. Now, the kind of attention that Sikh parents give their children seems to compare well with that given in reasonably favourable 'British' homes—the children are with mother all the time, and there is plenty of verbal play—'talking to baby', stories, nursery rhymes or lullabies. But the language is, of course, Punjabi. The implications of this are very important: Punjabi is, for these children, the language of their 'baby talk', the language in which they communicate to their mothers their most basic needs and feelings; the 'mother-tongue' is likely to remain for them the most vivid and eloquent way in which they can express their deepest emotions. It is the language in which they will communicate with members of their family and their community, unless, in later life, they break away from their powerful control in a very drastic manner, for example, by marrying someone of a different nationality and religion. It will be the language they use to talk about the features of home life that are distinctively 'Punjabi', the food they eat, the clothes they wear (in the case of girls and women, anyway) and—in the form of mutually intelligible Hindi or Urdu, of the films, music and broadcasts— the language of a significant part of their entertainment. And it is the language of the *Guru Granth Saheb* (although the dialects in which it is written are archaic and not easy to understand, like the English of the Authorized Version of the Bible, or more, that of Wyclif's) of the hymns and prayers, and of all that goes on in the *Gurdwara*.

It is necessary to emphasize these points, because there is a danger that the importance of Punjabi in the life of these children will be underestimated. From an 'English' standpoint, the need to know and use the language of the larger community seems so obvious and overriding that its limitations are overlooked. For a Sikh child, Punjabi is the code that he needs in order to function in his immediate environment—family community, *Gurdwara*, cinema. It may be largely a language of 'reinforcement'—casual conversation, jokes, politeness, and conveying factual information about everyday life. In these functions, it corresponds to the 'restricted codes' used by monolingual English speakers in a sub-stantial part of their day-to-day communication. Of course, Punjabi can also be used as an eloquent means of 'elaborating'—conveying new ideas, asking incisive, critical questions, providing an accurate and well-organized means of expression, and a tool for 'internal mediation' of problems, reasoning and understanding; it is likely that, by the time many Sikh children begin to learn English, they will have begun to learn to use Punjabi for such relatively sophisticated purposes. But primarily, Punjabi in Britain is a language for living within a community, sustaining and reinforcing its religious, social and moral traditions as well as its organization of day-to-day life. In effect, it is possible to live within this com-munity, perhaps quite happily, without ever learning any English —certainly any for active use, learning to speak English; many 'first generation' immigrants, particularly women, have managed to live in such a way.

However, they are very much dependent on others to interpret (both in the sense of translating and making intelligible) between them and the public services they need to resort to—shops, other than Indian food and dress shops, doctors, bus conductors, electri-cians, plumbers and so on. Children are, in many cases, growing up in this role of interpreter for their mothers, and this in itself must increase their awareness of the differences and ambivalent relations between their own community and 'English' society at large. The need for interpreters, and the power that knowledge of English gives to a member of the immigrant community, attaches prestige to the language which reinforces the idea, still very much present in India, that knowledge of English is a necessary mark of an educated person.

Sikh children enter nursery or infants schools knowing a certain amount of English—largely 'content words', names of things, actions or qualities, and a few colloquial expressions picked up in play with children in the neighbourhood or older brothers and sisters. A few seem quite 'fluent', but in most cases, even the talkative child strings together content words in a form of pidgin English which is structured only sufficiently to make sense in the immediate situation. In fact, if a child has 'learnt English' at home, it can be harmful in two ways—it might mean that he is unable to communicate effectively in his 'mother tongue', so that there is the beginning of a gulf of misunderstanding between the child and his mother, and it may hide the fact from his teachers that he really needs a great deal of specialized help with the English language. It will not be sufficient for these children to know just enough English to 'survive' in school—to obey orders, to give the occasional one-word answer to satisfy teacher in response to a simple, 'close-ended' question, and to understand roughly what is going on in the classroom. The English language must develop a whole new element in their consciousness and so in their personalities. If they are to succeed in school, they will need to use English as an instrument of reasoning—it will be a handicap if they have to think things out in a language different from that of their teachers, constantly switching mentally from one code to another, and, anyway, it is unlikely that a five-year-old will have developed a great deal of sophistication in the mother-tongue. In the process of learning in school, the child will have to listen to information and ideas expressed in English; he will have to make sense of this stream of language, understanding not only the words, but the significance of their order and context, selecting what information is relevant and important, noticing similarities and differences amongst pieces of information and so categorizing them and developing new concepts; he will be expected to draw conclusions from all this, and to apply the information to solving new problems, presenting his conclusions and solutions in a precise and well-supported manner. In effect, he has to learn not just a new language, but new, more sophisticated uses of language—the child who speaks English as his mother-tongue has, of course, to learn these new uses, too, but the bilingual child has a double problem.

Sikh parents have shown considerable enthusiasm for nursery education for their children—unfortunately, places are not available for all the children whose parents want them to have nursery education. Several who cannot get to nursery schools attend play-groups. Nursery classes and playgroups give these children excellent opportunities for play and for contact with other children and adults—opportunities much wider than the home can offer. On the other hand, as we have shown, the typical Sikh child grows up in a stable, secure environment in which he has plenty of encouragement and opportunity to learn. Nursery schooling is not needed for these children—as it is for some—on the grounds that the parents are unable, because of mental, social or financial difficulties, to bring up their own children and give them a fair start. There is no pressing 'social' need for nursery schooling for Sikh children.

The nursery schools will help the Sikh children to achieve the 'survival' level of competence in English that we described—enough 'content words' and a repertoire of colloquial phrases to enable them to 'survive' in the company of English-speaking children and adults. Can they do any more than this? At three years old, the child is still learning basic concepts—basic information about similarities and differences amongst the things and events he observes; his conceptual patterns are still being established, and they are established in terms of the patterns of meaning and construction of the mother-tongue. Use of a second language at this early age might create confusion and lack of fluency in either language. However, a child who enters the infants school with only 'survival competence' is at a serious disadvantage, and it is possible that the activities of a nursery school might be structured in such a way that systematic language-training could be given in the course of play-activities, concentrating on more sophisticated uses of language—for example, expression of relationships in space, talking about past or future events, describing things in terms of colour, shape, size, and comparing them. Experiments are being carried out on various techniques for developing the use of English (rather than simply 'knowledge' of English) amongst young children, and it is possible that effective techniques will be developed which may increase the child's ability to reason and to learn in both languages, rather than confusing him.

In the infants schools there is certainly need for systematic help with language;[1] bilingual children need training by specialist teachers with training in language-teaching techniques. Such specialists are used flexibly within the schools with a variety of children needing language-help; arrangements depend on the situation in each school—the type and number of the children's language-problems, availability of room, possibility of team teaching (the language development specialist teaching a group of children within a class, is in many ways the most satisfactory arrangement for young children for there is no need to take them away from the free and challenging environment of the infants classroom). The children, if they are to succeed, need to know how to ask—for things or for information—and how to answer,

[1] See the three articles in *English for Immigrants* (4:2), referred to in Biblio graphy, section 11.

giving the information they want to convey in a precise fashion, describing accurately, giving instructions, expressing their feelings. In order to do this, they need a register of English sufficiently precise and versatile, a rich vocabulary, and an understanding of and ability to use correctly the full grammatical repertoire of 'standard' English—distinctions of time, of number and sex, systems of cross-reference (nouns, verbs and pronouns) a variety of pre-positions, co-ordinating and subordinating connectives, comparison and various means of modifying noun and verb phrases. If specialist teachers work in infants schools, giving children training in these skills, they can help not only the children of non-English-speaking parents, but a great many monolingual English-speaking children too, to understand, think about, and participate in all that goes on in school. The children are involved in the full range of interesting and meaningful activities done in a good infants class, receiving such training as they need to be able to participate confidently, but at the same time the specialist teacher takes every opportunity to elicit acceptable forms of English, paying attention to different points of difficulty from time to time and arranging the activities so as to focus on particular points of language.

What we have said suggests a clear division of functions between Punjabi and English—the mother-tongue serving as the language of friendly intercourse, with family and other Sikhs, and as the language with the strongest emotional overtones for him, while English is the language of school, work, and communication with the 'impersonal' world of business and public services. Up to a point, this is a possible situation: everybody has a range of 'registers' and 'codes' of language which are used in different circumstances and for different purposes; for most of us, they are varying forms and usages of one language, but for the bi-lingual, they are forms of two different languages. For the first-generation immigrant, it is possible to make this distinction quite clearly and simply, but for his children the lines are much more blurred.

The Sikh child in school learns not only the formal English language used by teachers and by children talking with their teachers, but also the registers of the playground—'restricted codes' that sustain and reinforce the highly conservative child-community, lubricating, as it were, the machinery of that society. It is not just a matter of acquiring the pronunciation of the local accent, the distinctive structure and vocabulary of the local dialect, the appropriate curses and expletives, though these are all involved—the whole structure, intonation, pattern of gestures, and—to a considerable extent—even the content is strictly determined. In learning these kinds of language-behaviour, the children are beginning to play roles in society of which few of their parents were capable: for the first generation, casual conversation in

English is very much restricted and generally rather formal—sufficient chat with workmates to be polite and avoid conflict, probably less still with neighbours and anyone else. The possibility of close friendship, of being included in a group of English friends, is not great (there are, of course, exceptions, notably those early immigrants who had less of a community of their own to move in, and some of whom married English girls). But the child who grows up here learns what forms of language—and what forms of behaviour in general—are acceptable to other children, and so can 'make friends' with them. The young Sikh child in a nursery school or infants school plays with English-speaking children at playtime; however, if his competence in English is limited, he is likely to find himself almost always in the position of 'follower', being 'led' and instructed by native English-speakers. This cannot be a satisfactory situation for either party—the 'white' child will come to think that 'coloureds' are naturally in this inferior role, and he may well become frustrated if his attempts to instruct are not successful, so that the multi-racial play situation will break down.[1] The answer is systematic language teaching for the young bilinguals, coupled with some supervised 'practice in playing' playground games in playgroups, nursery schools and infants schools. As time goes on, they learn other registers—for speaking politely to unknown adults, for speaking with varying degrees of familiarity, for making formal statements, for speaking angrily, and so on; language-learning is a process of increasing 'involvement' in the community. Learning the language appropriate for different social situations is an important element in language training, and systematic help can be given in role-play activities, stories, games with puppets and so on.

But the process is not a smooth one, and the child may be pulled two ways. Young Sikh children begin to use English in their own play, in talking to their brothers and sisters; their Punjabi becomes loaded with English loanwords—primarily the names of things and institutions peculiar to British society, but also substituting for things that could as well be expressed in Punjabi, to such a degree that elderly relatives coming from India complain that they cannot understand the Punjabi of these children. In school the children are discouraged from speaking Punjabi, and rewarded for speaking English (with teacher's approval, and awareness of success); they may come to feel that there is something definitely 'wrong' about speaking Punjabi, that it is a mark of ignorance.

They learn, of course, to read and write in English. The systematic training in language which we have described precedes and complements the normal pre-reading and initial reading train-

[1] See Eileen Lucas on 'Language in the Infants Playground', *Multiracial School* (1:3; 2:1), Bibliography, section 11.

ing given in infants schools. Sikh children respond well, in general, to a fairly formal introduction to reading, though there is a danger that if they develop decoding ('phonic') skills very efficiently that they will learn a habit of decoding mechanically without attention to meaning. From the start, and throughout the primary school, emphasis is needed on comprehension and on written work conforming to acceptable grammatical standards. When engaged in oral work in class, when answering a teacher's question for example, a child has to think both about the content of his answer and about the appropriate grammatical structure of the answer; in written work, there is the further problem of spelling and formation of letters. The use of exercises like 'filling in blanks' or writing essays, letters etcetera based on a 'model', is thought to be arid and hostile to creativity, but many children (not only bilinguals) may need the help of a 'framework', providing either the structure of a sentence, so that they have only to fill in the content-words, or the other way about. If such 'frameworks' are given not as meaningless drills, but as an aid to talking and writing about information learnt in interesting 'discovery' activities—topics, experiments, field-studies and so on—they can be a great help to the 'linguistically handicapped' child; of course, as time goes on, the 'props' can gradually be removed until the child is able to compose quite freely. The presence of children with obvious language difficulties in schools has drawn attention to the less apparent difficulties of many monolingual English-speakers, and to the need to reconsider the language involved in the whole range of school work—the language of mathematical and scientific ideas, of history, literature and the other 'humanities' and of technical instruction.

Sikh children buy English comics, and, if they have any books of their own (many do have) they are likely to be English books —fairy stories, Enid Blyton, Ladybird Books and educational textbooks bought by ambitious parents in an effort to help with their academic progress. Parents will have prayer-books in *Gurmukhi* scripts, and are likely to read the Punjabi newspapers published by immigrant groups in Southall, Gravesend and Birmingham, but it is unlikely that the children will be able to read them. Efforts are made at the *Gurdwara* to teach *Gurmukhi*; Sikhs who teach in local schools are capable teachers, and the children enjoy these lessons, but they are not experts at teaching reading, and there is no material available beyond the primers used in India. These compare ill with the English books that the children have at school, being cheaply produced in black and white (except for the first book); what is more, they contain a great deal that is unintelligible to a child who has grown up in Britain, although it would be everyday matter to children in the Punjab—camels, pomegranates, mangoes, ploughshares, buffaloes, butter-churns, sugarcane and maize. In effect, few of them learn more than the names of the letters of the *Gurmukhi* alphabet; fortunately, the spelling system is fairly systematic, and this knowledge may be adequate to enable them to decode, but there is little to motivate them to learn to read or write fluently in their mother-tongue.

On the other hand, as they grow older, they must become aware—as we have been showing—that they are 'different'; moreover, their contemporaries become aware of this fact, too. We do not know very much as yet about the way in which children's attitudes develop to other people and other groups of people. It becomes apparent when children reach adolescence if they have learnt to accept the myths and stereotypes of the groups to which they belong, or if they have learnt to suspend judgement and weigh evidence before coming to conclusions. But how do these attitudes develop? More important than what children—of 6 years old, 11 or 14—say about people of other races, religions or classes, is the habit of thinking that has led them to these conclusions.

We understand much better now than a generation ago how mathematical and scientific concepts develop in the minds of children; as a result, children in Junior and even Infants schools are working with ideas in mathematics, physics and other sciences which were formely not introduced below university level. Perhaps equally rigorous thinking is needed in respect of the 'humanities', the curricular subjects which involve the study of other human beings, and of ourselves. The traditional studies—geography, history, literature, religious studies—need to be reconsidered at very least to give a fairer picture of the achievements past and present of civilizations and cultures other than our own. The Punjab is a particularly exciting place at the present time on account of remarkable progress in agriculture and the growth of light industries; in history, it was a meeting place of civilizations comparable to the Middle East; the Sikh religion is worthy of serious consideration amongst the great religions of the world; and we have hinted at the wealth of story, music, dance, costume and cuisine that are elements in the home life of Sikh children. Yet many of them attend schools where these things never are mentioned— India is a 'backward country', its history only mentioned as a series of British conquests and native rebellions, its religions superstitious paganism, its culture an obscure backwater. Syllabi for G.C.E. and C.S.E. papers in these subjects reflect and reinforce this attitude; textbooks continue to retail these myths.

The study of world history and comparative religion, the fairer treatment of the developing countries in geography, the introduction of Punjabi music, cookery, dressmaking, stories or festivals would all enrich the life of a school, remove some hoary preconceptions, and enable Sikh children to feel that they have something to 'give' and be proud of, instead of always 'receiving' and 'being helped'. We have hinted in our account of the life of the children at the rich, living culture of the Sikh community; there are opportunities here to enrich the life of all children in our schools and of the community. But there are some basic conflicts between the expectations and values of Sikh parents and the values inculcated in our schools—we have tried to describe, and have perhaps caricatured, the Sikh parents' view of the role of a school, and mentioned how the beliefs and standards of behaviour of the community are taken for granted, being inculcated at home by force of example. Our schools, with their tradition of 'humane', 'liberal' education place high value on individual initiative, independent decision-making, freedom and privacy—ideas that can be directly in conflict with *sewa* in the sense of duty to the family and community, upholding communal traditions without question, accepting and performing one's *Dharam*. Sikh parents do not object to their children learning about Christianity, and do not ask for their children to be withdrawn from school assemblies or religious instruction. There have been demands for separate religious instruction, but these have so far been made only by a few Sikh politicians and have not been supported by any genuine requests from ordinary Sikh parents. Of course, separate religious instruction might help in encouraging young people to have pride in their community's traditions, but it is not really the answer to the fundamental conflict of values, and may prove counter-productive; in a rapidly changing, pluralistic society, no children can be 'insulated' from challenges and alternatives to the accepted beliefs of their parents, and attempts at indoctrination are unlikely to have the desired effect.

Perhaps we need to look more deeply, and consider what basic ideas about human society young children can and should grasp—perhaps the basic ideas of some subjects not yet in the school curriculum: sociology, anthropology, community studies, comparative religion? Children in junior schools learn about their environment; they note old and new buildings, the types of trees and birds, but what do they learn about their human environment? They learn that people in different parts of the world live in different kinds of houses—do they know why these houses are different, how each type is best suited to its particular environment? More important, what is common and what is distinctive to what goes on inside these houses? The idea that communities are different from each other without being 'better' or 'worse' than one another is basic. So is the idea that 'family', 'home', 'friend', 'God', 'good' may mean rather different things to different people, yet these ideas have much in common, and one interpretation may not necessarily be more 'right' than another.

As things are, very young children are certainly aware of physical differences amongst individuals and groups of people, and junior-age children talk quite knowledgeably about differences of social custom—food, clothes, religious practices. The origins of prejudice and conflict are early in life, even if there is little apparent tension in Primary schools. The attitudes that adolescents reveal—at the same stage in life as they begin to judge and criticize attitudes—are established much earlier in life. But it is in Secondary schools, and when they come to leave school, that the progress that young Sikhs have made in learning to 'get on' with other children is likely to meet with checks, and they may turn to the company of the exclusive groups of Punjabi-speaking friends. Such peer-groups of Sikh youths are likely to have an important role, in the lives of the members and in the development of the émigré community. Their influence is likely to be basically 'conservative', sustaining the sense of belonging to a distinctive community but if they adopt the trappings of a partly Western 'teenage culture', parents will regard them as rebellious and subversive elements. At the same time, the teenager becomes increasingly aware of the demands of the wider society, and especially of the need for a good standard of spoken English when seeking prestigious skilled, white-collar or professional jobs. Paradoxically, their desire to fulfil their own parents' ambitions for them may be a greater influence towards 'anglicization' than their desire to identify with a 'rebellious' teenage peer-group.

7 Growing Up

Young people in our Western society are faced with a number of very serious choices when they reach their majority—in particular, they have a relatively wide choice regarding whom they will marry and when, and regarding what career they will follow. Besides these, there are choices of religious or political persuasion that many young people take quite seriously. The young Sikh living in the traditional village environment is relieved of much of this decision-making by the family and the social system—his or her marriage-partner is chosen by parents and elders, jobs are, traditionally at least, determined to a large extent by the social position of the family, religious and political loyalties are very much taken for granted, and young people are expected to conform to their norms without questioning.

In Britain, of course, the young Sikhs are aware that there are many other communities, religions and political creeds besides those of their parents, and they must see the relative 'freedom' of choice that young people in Britain exercise in their lives. Serious tensions between the second generation and the first seem almost inevitable in this situation. But it is not a straightforward matter of the young people rejecting the values of their elders and adopting a set of values learnt from their contemporaries. The young Sikh who does not conform in some way—symbolic, like cutting his hair, or more drastically still by refusing to leave the choice of a marriage-partner to his parents—cannot be sure that he will find acceptance in the 'white' community: the family and community may be oppressive, but they provide security. The teenager who finds himself rejected by his white contemporaries, or by the social system in general is as likely to revert to extreme identification with the distinctive community, asserting his identity as a Sikh in every possible way. A Sikh boy or girl 'cut off' from the community because of some refusal to conform has little to fall back on, and their upbringing is such that they are likely to be very dependent—in India, this can result in prolonged immaturity; one reads newspaper reports about 'a boy of 30' or 'a youth of 35', still, presumably, subject to the discipline of his father and very much dependent on the affection of his mother. One cannot tell how many young Sikhs feel that, in conforming to their parents' expectations at least at home and behaving as they are required to, they are being consciously hypocritical for the sake of a quiet life. Some certainly admit to having such feelings. On the other hand, a young Sikh brought up in a partly 'anglicized' home in Kenya, said that, after trying to make friends with young English people without success, he felt that he wanted to 'serve his own people'; he had started to attend the *Gurdwara* for the first time in his life. They all have (like anyone else) different 'identities' in different social environments; with English contemporaries they are one thing, at home they may be quite different. But for most, the 'home' identity, the Punjabi in them, is probably the most 'real'.

But this impression of prolonged immaturity is offset by the fact that quite young children are entrusted with quite considerable responsibilities in the home—looking after baby, helping with decoration or repairs, acting as interpreter in shops and public offices, shopping and paying bills. They are expected to be able to fend for themselves to a fair extent in the home, to use money sensibly, and the fact of having what—from the parents' point of view—are limitless educational opportunities, must place a great burden of anxiety on them, and a sense of great responsibility to achieve. Alienation from their white contemporaries and lack of freedom to do anything much except study may aggravate an over-anxious, grimly determined attitude to school or college work. Children have clearly defined roles within the family; in some respects, graduation to adulthood comes very young, in others, it is much delayed, by comparison with western patterns. The traditional culture recognizes no 'in between' stage of 'teenage culture', the roles of children and adults are closely and organically inter-linked. This is not to say that Sikh parents are unaware of adolescence as a stormy period in life: the seven years or so after puberty (*jawa*, Sanskrit *yuva*) are talked of as a troubled period when contradictory elements in the personality—conflicting ideas, feelings and aspirations—are in fierce 'battle'.

The young Sikh in Britain develops, in consequence, a rather ambivalent outlook—very much attached to home, a symbol of security for him, and the supportive family and community social system which are valuable psychological props yet drawn to reject these by the example of his non-Sikh peers. Moreover, the position of the parents, the first generation, is not simple; they themselves have made a great and difficult 'break' in migrating, and they may have much sympathy with the frustration and rebelliousness of their sons and daughters, but they are themselves subject to pressure from their elders—the grandparents, aunts, and purveyors of village gossip back in the Punjab. They, too, are afraid to commit themselves to a complete rejection of these links, that are fundamental elements in their own personalities, the basic motivation for almost anything they do or any decision they make.

For the elders in the Punjab, and for the more conservative of the first generation in Britain, the way of life of Western industrial cities is extravagant, immoral, unhealthy, and above all, fraught with insecurity and loneliness—in youth and old age, at work, and in the neighbourhood. The community approves of 'simplicity'—if you are said to be 'simple-minded', it is meant as a compliment, while 'sophisticated' and 'fashionable' are terms implying some disapproval. Young people are criticized severely for spending money 'frivolously', on clothes, records and suchlike. Yet young Sikhs are expected to be highly ambitious. In practice, they have proved capable of adapting to the requirements of societies different from their own, and to jobs requiring skills that are very different from those developed in the Punjabi village. The parents may not realize how strong their children's loyalty to family and religion may still be.

The greatest tension seems likely to develop as a result of the marriage system, and the marked differences between Sikh and Western societies in their attitude to women and girls; the teenage girls will probably face greater problems than their brothers. We have mentioned that, unlike the men, the girls and women continue to dress in the Punjabi costume of *kamiz* and *shalwar*: this fact is in itself significant—the women are the guardians of the values and traditions of the community, and great importance is attached to their maintaining these traditions. It is important to dismiss any idea that women are regarded by Sikhs as 'inferior' members of the community, or that they are simply kept in subjection by the men. We have already suggested that Sikh boys are inclined sometimes to be dominated by their mothers, and in later life they may be subject to hen-pecking from their wives (though psychological compensation may create an opposite tendency). The men are expected to be active: as breadwinners, as the spokesmen of the family in dealing with outsiders, and in the 'official' organizations of the community. But a woman has considerable authority within her own household: she has the last word on many matters, especially those related to the upbringing of her children; she is consulted by her husband with regard to any matter that affects the whole family and her word carries much weight.

The Sikhs pride themselves on their relatively progressive attitude to the position of women in society.[1] The teachings of the Gurus on this subject amount to a rejection of the negative aspects of Hindu and Muslim traditions, in particular the idea that women are 'unclean', prone to sinfulness, inherently weak-minded and created mainly as a temptation by the Almighty:

> It is by woman, the 'condemned' one, that we are conceived and from her that we are born; it is with her that we are betrothed and married.

[1] See the article by G. S. Sidhu referred to in section 6 of the Bibliography.

It is woman we befriend, it is she who keeps the race going.
When one woman dies, we seek another; it is with her that we
    become established in society.
Why should we call her 'inferior', who gives birth to great men?
A woman is born of a woman, none is born without a woman.
O Nanak, only the Lord has no need for a woman.

                              (*Asa di Var*, MI, p. 475.)

Guru Har Gobind described woman as 'the conscience of man'.
Immoral or irresponsible behaviour in a woman is regarded as
much more serious than such behaviour in a man. In a sense, this
suggests that society attributes greater importance to women than
to men, but it means that women have a greater burden of responsibility and so their freedom is more restricted. Although there was
no woman Guru, women played a very active part in the development of the religion and community, even to the extent of fighting
in the armies of the *Khalsa*. Legends of women saints and heroes
are an element in popular tradition that must encourage the
formation of a fairly positive view of women—Mata Sundri, Mai
Bhago and Satwant Kaur are well-known examples. Women are
admitted to *Gurdwaras* on equal terms, and more often than not
they are in a majority in the *Sangat*; they can and do serve as
Granthis or amongst the '*Panch Piare*' in ceremonies, preach, recite
and serve as officers in the *Gurdwara* and the higher levels of
Sikh organization, such as the *Shiromani Gurdwara Parbandhak
Committee*, but more characteristically they let the men act as
spokesmen, though they make their views known on any matter
under discussion.

In fact, the teachings of the Gurus emphasized the positive
aspects of the Hindu tradition, especially reverence for woman
as mother, and as the main agent for maintaining the traditions
of the community and passing on religious and ethical teaching
from one generation to another. Thus, the stereotype of the shy
and submissive Indian women is hardly truthful in the case of the
Sikh *Kaurs*. But it must be observed that these religious and social
traditions do not necessarily inculcate reverence for woman as a
person in society—they certainly do not mean 'emancipation' in
the sense that it is understood here, though some Sikh apologists
equate the two points of view. Reverence for woman as mother
can still mean that she is regarded primarily as a producer of
sons, essentially dependent and expected to 'worship' her husband
irrespective of his character. In the common law of the Punjab, the
joint property of the extended family is held in the name of the
men of the family, and daughters do not inherit or transmit any
part of it (except their dowries and rights to income from it if all
men in the family die).

And the fact remains that, when a girl is born, the parents do
not celebrate; girls are still regarded as a liability—mainly, as

we shall see, because of the economics of the marriage system.[1]
We have described already how little girls graduate at quite an
early age from imitating their mothers in play to actually helping
them and working in the home. They perform quite a heavy load
of domestic duties, and at the same time learn from their mothers
and sisters the range of domestic skills that a girl is expected to
have acquired by the time she is marriageable. This is not to say
that the girls are ill-treated or neglected in favour of their brothers.
They are generally indulgently treated with presents and new
clothes, and, as they get older, it may be that parents try by
material generosity to offset the restrictions on a girl's behaviour
that they believe to be necessary.

A marriage is arranged between the parents of the boy and the
girl. Generally, they will choose a partner of the same 'tribe' (i.e.
Jat, Ramgarhia, Khatri, etc.) but of a different *goth*; some *goths*
have traditional marriage-links with others, but there is no rigid
pattern. A *Jat* man married a *Ramgarhia* girl, and this was disapproved of by a section of his family (his father's brother and
his immediate family); this led to violent quarrelling in the family,
ending with a fight in which the man killed his uncle. This means,
invariably, that a partner is found from a different village from
that where the family belongs. It is considered desirable that the
boy and girl should not have known each other before the marriage.
In the Punjab, this means that parents with a son or daughter to
be married will seek a partner amongst families of the same tribe,
of a different *goth* from their own or their parents (but possibly
of certain specified other *goths* of the same tribe), in a circle of
villages within riding distance but beyond walking distance of
their own (this is because it is considered undesirable for the couple
to have met before, even by chance; within the village, *Jat* families
will generally be of the same or a closely related *goth* and regarded
as 'kin' to the extent of calling each other by terms of family
relationship—*phra, phaenji, dada*, etc.). Parents are, of course, very
concerned that unfavourable rumours about the characters of their
sons and (especially) daughters should not circulate in these
villages—a fear that influences their attitude to their children's
behaviour. A father who warned his daughter when she went to
college that, if she dragged his name in the dirt, he would kill her
first and then kill himself, was probably not exaggerating. While
physical punishment and cruelty are not common, when family
honour and everything a Sikh believes in seem to be threatened,
the reaction may be very violent.

In practice, parents in village 'A' will expect their sons to marry
girls from a fairly limited selection in one of a few villages—'BCD',

---

[1] See *An Indian Girl growing up in Britain*, in Bibliography, section 6. I
was greatly helped in this account of the problems faced by Sikh girls by the
frank comments of the author of that article.

but will look for husbands for their daughters in a different range of villages 'EFG'.[1] *Jat* Sikhs rarely marry Hindus, even *Jat* Hindus.

The parents will look for other features besides tribe and family. Some make a point of comparing the horoscopes of their child with that of the prospective partner, others make more practical enquiries about education, financial status or health record. The character of the boy or girl is considered—value is placed on 'simplicity' rather than 'sophistication'. The character of the family or prospective in-laws is also considered, especially for the sake of the girl who is going to have to live with them and be subject to their will. They, conversely, will want her to be willing to serve not only her husband, but to take her share in cooking, washing, caring for children and for the sick and old of the whole family. Traditionally, the boy and girl were not supposed to meet at all before marriage, though nowadays, amongst Sikhs in Britain, it is not uncommon for a chaperoned meeting to be arranged where they can at least look at each other. Photos are also exchanged, if the marriage is being arranged between partners in Britain and India or elsewhere in the world, though conservative families regard this as bad form. Beauty is judged chiefly in terms of height and skin colour—a moderately tall, fair-skinned boy or girl is regarded as the ideal. But the biggest consideration is financial. A dowry is invariably a part of the marriage-bargain, and is likely to remain, as there is no other automatic inheritance that a girl can expect from her parents. There are sad stories of girls married simply for the sake of their money, and as long as parents have to 'buy' husbands for their daughters, girls will be considered a liability. Dowries range from £150 upwards amongst Sikhs in Britain, but are commonly in excess of £400 and can run into thousands. The cost of the wedding has to be borne by the bride's family, and this can be correspondingly excessive.

Families in Britain may still make their first enquiries about partners for their children in the same quarter, the 'circle' of villages near their own—or amongst people from those villages who have settled in Britain. If a boy in Britain is to marry a girl from the Punjab, he will expect to bring her to Britain. As the Immigration Laws stand, though, it is impossible for girls to 'import' husbands in this way. This creates a grave problem for these girls—while there are plenty of Sikh boys in Britain, their parents demand very high dowries, and they have the option of 'importing' daughters of wealthy families in India. Girls from India are considered preferable marriage partners for their sons by conservative parents who suspect that girls brought up in England will be rebellious and discontented wives, and that (as they will have grown up in divided, 'nucleated' families) they will

[1] See the articles by Mrs. M. Smith in Bibliography, section 6.

be less willing to share in family duties. Girls from India will, of course, usually have a mother-in-law in Britain, so the sheltered environment of the Punjabi household will be recreated even more faithfully for these girls than it could have been for the 'first generation'. If the 'importation' of wives from the Punjab continues as a regular pattern, they will become a very important conservative influence in the community, maintaining religious and social traditions and offsetting the 'Westernized' character of their British Sikh husbands.

Conversely, some Sikh girls who have been in Britain for many years, even girls born in Britain, may be under pressure to return to India to marry; this pressure is likely to be greatest if the parents suspect that the girl has become too 'Westernized' in her ways. The Sikh political leaders have campaigned with petitions and demonstrations for a change in the law relating to immigration by wives, husbands, fiancés and fiancées. There is a feeling that, if there has to be a ban on entry, it had better apply to women as well as to men, so as to rectify the 'marriage market'.

Sikh parents are concerned that their daughters should get as good an education as their sons—this is no modern phenomenon, there were many schools for girls in the Punjab before it was invaded by the British in the 1840s. However, education is regarded, to some extent, as a way out of the vicious circle of the dowry system (as it also by-passes the caste system): an 'educated' girl can hope for a much better marriage than she would otherwise get with the dowry her parents could afford. There is difficulty here, too, for families in Britain: Sikh boys educated in Britain can command high dowries from their wives' families even if they leave school at the age of 16—they are as 'expensive' as graduates in India (the real difference in educational standards may not be as great as all that, but a 'degree', however insignificant, is perceived as a great asset).

Even if this is the main motive for getting girls educated, the fact that there is a class of educated women within the community is bound to be a factor bringing change; educated girls and women are not content to be mothers and nothing more, and they are likely to be agents of social reform within the community.

The ambitiousness of educated girls creates problems for their parents; traditionally, marriage arrangements were made as early as possible. Child-marriages were very common, though the 'marriage' was of course a formality, and a second marriage (*muklavan*) was celebrated when the couple were mature. When child-marriage was made illegal (1929), all that happened was substitution of a 'betrothal' ceremony for the actual 'marriage'. The 'betrothal' ceremony settles the arrangement between the parents—the girl's parents bring presents to the boy's home and are entertained there (this, of course, means a flight to India if the girl is to marry a boy there). There is not much sign of early betrothals being arranged by Sikh parents in Britain, though, and the girls prefer to delay as late as possible. The age of twenty-five, after they have completed their education, and possibly established themselves in some job, would be acceptable. Moreover, the longer the girl stays at school or college, the more concerned her parents become about the likelihood of contact with boys, and of the influence of Western morality.

In practice, parents are more often than not willing to listen to the views of their sons and daughters about when they will marry and what sort of person they will marry, as far as the communal traditions allow. I know of many cases where parents have been persuaded to delay marriage until their son or daughter completed education or started a career, and of cases where an arrangement that was being negotiated was vetoed because the boy or girl was not happy with the prospect—especially when a girl was going to have to go to India. The most rigid and uncompromising parents are not necessarily those who adhere very strictly to traditional conventions in their own lives. Some of the most serious conflicts between Sikh parents and children arise when the parents' own attitude to Western morality is ambivalent, or when there is disagreement between mother and father. The right of 'veto' is fairly generally recognized, and parents may even accept suggestions from their children if the proposed partner meets their requirements; in such a way, a kind of 'love-marriage' might be acceptable within the 'arranged' framework.

The marriage ceremony is performed at the bride's home, or (more usually in Britain) at the nearest *Gurdwara*. The groom is supposed to bathe in scented water, then he is dressed in his best clothes with a pink or red turban from which gold streamers hang down over his face (these seem to be done without in Britain); he is garlanded with flowers and relations give him presents of money as he sets off with a party of relations and friends (the *Barat*) to the wedding; when he arrives he sits at the *Gurdwara*. Presents are exchanged between the fathers of the couple; the bride's parents are responsible for entertaining the groom's party before as well as after the wedding. All the immediate relatives of the bride and groom have various jobs to do at the wedding and in the preparations beforehand; this is true even when the family is split up and members have to travel from overseas to attend.

The ceremony (*Anand Karaj*) is basically quite a simple one, being an adaption of the Hindu wedding (where the couple walk around the sacred fire) to the character of the Sikh religion, with its rejection of idolatry and supreme reverence for the *Guru Granth Saheb*. If, as is generally the case, the wedding is on a Sunday, it is performed during the regular Sunday morning

Assembly, in the presence of the *Sangat*. The bride comes in beautifully dressed in red or pink, with her head (and traditionally her face too) covered, and jewels on her face, neck, hands and feet; she sits on the left of the groom. The ceremony begins with prayers, recitation of certain *Shabads*, and delivery by the *Granthi* of a series of instructions to newly-weds. Then the *Anand Saheb* is sung. The climax of the ceremony, and the moment sometimes fixed by consulting an astrologer, is the *Lavan*, when the groom leads the bride four times round the *Guru Granth Saheb*, as the four verses of the marriage-hymn of Guru Ram Das (*Lavan Suhi*, M IV, p. 773) are sung. During the fourth round the guests throw flower-petals or confetti. Money is also thrown, though this is disapproved of and attempts have been made to forbid it. The difficulty that faces any attempt to encourage 'simplicity' in weddings is that the parents of any girl who is about to be married resent being the ones to set an example of 'simplicity'. Attempts to reduce extravagance in weddings have been characteristic of 'reform' movements in the Punjab from the time of the Gurus onward, and were certainly a feature of the revival of Sikh religion early this century. The influence of Western customs might encourage similar movements in Britain, but only a strong *Gurdwara* Management Committee could introduce such reforms; in a situation where there are no generally accepted 'leaders' and a multiplicity of personal and family rivalries, such changes are unlikely.

After the religious ceremony, there is a party at the bride's home, or in a hired hall; the groom's father inspects the dowry, if it includes chattels of any kind. Elders of both families and honoured guests make speeches, there are folk-songs and dances, recitation of songs and poems, and the jollifications continue well into the night or even for several days. There is a curious tradition, *Sithnian*, whereby the groom has to sit and try to keep a straight face while the female relatives of the bride sing songs, tease him and try to make him laugh—they usually succeed, and shower him with presents.

The departure of the bride (still heavily veiled) and groom is accompanied by traditional songs and dances (*Doli*); this is the moment in her life when a Sikh girl is, for the first time, completely alone, leaving the security of her parents' home to live with people that she has probably never met; this must be quite shattering— the emotion is eloquently expressed in the great ballad *Doli charhdian mariyan Heer cheekan* referred to in Chapter 5; it is taken for granted that the bride and her mother and other female relatives will break down and cry at this point, if not before. In a traditional wedding, the bride and groom do not see each other until they reach the groom's home, where the groom's mother unveils the bride rather like unwrapping a parcel.

The system of arranged marriages does, in fact, ensure a fair likelihood of compatibility, social and intellectual—and most parents do their best to ensure a happy marriage for their children, though their ideas of their children's best interests may be coloured by their own social aspirations. There certainly are some unhappy marriages—a girl may not like the man her parents choose for her, still less his mother or sister. The Sikhs point with some pride to the fact that few such marriages break up completely, but this is mainly because divorce is not approved of (in this respect, the Sikhs are more conservative than the Muslims) and the chances of a divorced woman remarrying or spending any but a miserable life are very limited. On the other hand, there are unmarried girls who get fed up with the stifling atmosphere of their own family, and long for a husband to take them away from it—cases where a girl is being kept unmarried to nurse her parents, for example. The unhappiness both of the wife who longs for her parents' home and of the girl who longs for a husband is expressed in many Punjabi folk-songs.

The position of widows is not very satisfactory, although the social teaching of the Sikh Gurus aimed at improving their unhappy position. When a husband dies, his widow is expected to break up her bangles, dress in white, and live 'on sufferance' with her in-laws. However, she is entitled to keep her own property, and her dowry reverts to her. Few Sikh women have been widowed in Britain, but one or two have chosen to remain here taking factory jobs, living alone with their children (in one case, two widows share a council house), depending on relatives of their own or their husband's who are in this country to help and support them. Few widows, however young, are likely to be able to remarry. On the other hand, young widowers generally remarry as soon as they can. This can lead to difficulties for the children of the first marriage, as their stepmother may not feel obliged to act as their protector and 'advocate' as their real mother would, and may, indeed, be jealous of their seniority to her own children. In bad cases, two teenage boys were virtually 'rejected' by their father and young stepmother; the parents ultimately moved away to London, with the children of the second marriage, leaving the boys to find jobs and lodging and to fend for themselves; a girl of 11 was used very much as a 'servant' by her stepmother, who only allowed her to eat when all the rest of the family had finished. A woman deserted by her husband is also in an unhappy state, though she can (as a widow generally cannot) depend on her own relatives for help and support. Cases of desertion did arise during the upheaval of migration, though in most cases the wives remained with their families in India. The community at large (but not necessarily his own family) ostracize a man who deserts his wife, and even his own family blame him severely for bringing them into disrepute.

It is interesting that the classical legends of the Punjab, as well as the escapist fantasies of the Hindi cinema, very often relate to love between boy and girl, and the arranged marriage system is portrayed as, at best, a necessary evil, a kind of malignant fate overriding the wishes of 'star-crossed lovers'. Yet love-marriages are definitely 'unusual', and are frowned upon. But they are not that uncommon, especially amongst college-educated young people in India. Young Sikhs in Britain must at least be aware that they are the rule amongst their contemporaries here; this is a matter—along with job and educational aspirations, and religious conformity— on which young Sikhs are very likely to disagree seriously with their parents. In extreme cases, the possibility of running away from home arises; a girl who does this, of course, cuts herself off completely from her family and community, and must depend entirely on the loyalty of her boyfriend (coloured or white) and the willingness of the 'white' community to accept her. For the 'over-protective' atmosphere of home and her parents' uncompromising moral certainty she exchanges the insecurity and possible misery that is undeniably more prevalent amongst young people in the 'host community'—a greater danger of desertion, divorce, or being an unmarried mother, and the greater likelihood of financial hardship even if her boyfriend or husband remains loyal.

There is little sign that the 'arranged marriage' system will break down when the British-born Sikhs grow up: I came across second-generation Canadian-born Sikhs knowing no Punjabi who had travelled to India to marry girls selected by their families.[1] A significant number of young men immigrants formed liaisons with 'local' girls during the early sixties, and several mixed marriages have survived in happy stability. Once numbers of wives had come from India, the incidence of mixed marriages seemed to drop, but it is highly possible that young British Sikhs will form such attachments. Their parents are unlikely to approve, but the Sikh man who marries an English girl is not rejected by his family and community in the way that a Brahmin would be, especially if the girl adopts Punjabi habits of dress or food, and learns the language. The possibility of Sikh girls marrying English boys is, of course, much more remote, and would be much more likely to lead to her rejection by her family, not necessarily because her husband would be English, but such a marriage would be preceded by courtship; this is feared by Sikh parents as, if the courtship did *not* lead to marriage, the girl's chances of an arranged marriage would be gravely affected. This means that adolescent 'love affairs', a central feature of the white teenage culture and initiation to adulthood in Western society, are impossible for these girls. It must be a source of desperate frustration for them when they find that their friends

[1] See Rose *et al.*, *Colour and Citizenship*, p. 459. Bibliography, section 10.

at school are having such intense experiences which are denied to them.

Before marriage, a Sikh girl has reasonable freedom of behaviour, by comparison with a Muslim girl, though she cannot, of course, go out with boys, dance, drink or smoke. There is no bar on her speaking to men or boys, nor is she required to keep silent in the company of her elders. A young married woman is expected to be more retiring, to leave dealings with strangers, especially men, to her husband and in-laws, but if they are not present, she should be able to deal with them by herself. She will remain quiet in the presence of older people, especially her father- and mother-in-law, not sit when they are standing, and use the polite forms of Punjabi in addressing them. She will walk with her husband, not behind him as Muslim women do, and sit beside him at home when guests are entertained. There is no *purdah*, veiling of the face in public, and no objection to being photographed. Middle-aged and older women are less reserved in dealing with strangers, in speaking up in public meetings and at the *Gurdwara*, and are regarded with respect by younger people, men as well as women.

The Sikh girl is brought up to find fulfilment in having and caring for children—her place is certainly in the home. In Britain, this may mean that she is very much alone, with her husband and children away all day and no relatives—parents, aunts or sisters—for company. Punjabi village life is very much in the open-air: neighbours are met at the well, on the rooftop, or in the fields. Sikh women in Britain depend very much on any Punjabi neighbours for company, and resist any wish of their husbands to move away from the 'ghetto'.[1] Feelings vary with regard to women taking jobs. Girls are encouraged to 'qualify' for respectable professions —notably teaching; it is likely that there will be a steady stream of applicants for places in colleges of education from the Sikh community, at least in colleges near enough to home for the girls to attend as day students. Few girls have been allowed to go away to residential colleges, and mixed colleges are of course regarded with greater suspicion than the few single-sex ones. Nursing is also acceptable. Office work is regarded with suspicion by some parents—on the whole, they prefer that their daughters should avoid work where there is much social contact with men. They are pleased if they show ability in scientific studies, so that they can study at a technical college and possibly obtain skilled technical work—in industrial laboratories, for example. A number of older

---

[1] The traditional 'friendship group' of women (generally related to each other) is the 'girls of the spinning wheel' who meet together in each other's houses to chat as they spin and do other jobs. Groups of Sikh housewives who meet in each other's homes to gossip while their small children play together are developing a useful replacement for this group. They share not only gossip, but worries, sorrows and joys and provide mutual support. See J. S. Dosanjh, *Punjabi Immigrant Children in Britain*, Bibliography, section 11.

Sikh women immigrants, and probably more of their daughters, have taken semi-skilled jobs in the textile industry, mostly sewing and mending. These are taken to supplement the family income and as an escape from housebound loneliness, but this is disapproved of by more conservative Sikhs who consider it wrong for a *Jat* woman to be employed by anyone who is not a *Jat* (so they have no objection to girls and women—usually relatives—working for *Jat* shopkeepers as counter assistants). Most families where where wives or daughters are working (especially in factories or service industries) have concealed this fact from relatives in the Punjab, who would regard it as evidence of serious loss of status. Like the men, they have only the most superficial social contact with fellow-workers who are not Punjabis, speaking little English and not eating with them.

There are, in fact, two classes of Sikh working women; girls who have been to school in Britain and are waiting to marry (in the Punjab, such girls would generally have to stay at home), and older married women whose children are at school or grown up. Newly married brides and wives with infant children are expected to stay at home, often under the wing of mother-in-law. However, if they have professional training, they are more likely to continue working. It seems that young wives whose husbands' families have shops are allowed to work in these.

In our exploration of some aspects of the life of Sikh children in Britain, we have noticed many respects in which the life they lead is distinct from that of other children: 'symbolic' features, such as clothing and food, more profound features, such as beliefs about the Absolute, the meaning of 'home' and the family, features likely to be sources of tension, such as ideas of education or the marriage-system. The growing child must become increasingly aware of the fact of being 'different', from other children in school, from other people in the neighbourhood and of the hostility this 'difference' generates. His first loyalty is to his family, especially in the link with his mother, and to the extended family and the Sikh community, locally and universally, the *Khalsa Panth*. These children have particular, unique difficulties to face by reason of this distinctiveness; they can be helped in many ways by their teachers and other 'outside' agents if those people take the trouble to understand the background to their lives, without being too ready to pass judgement or jump to conclusions about it. But much can, and inevitably will be done to mould their personalities by their own people, the Sikh community; without the community, they are rootless, cut off from everything that has influenced their development in their early years. As they grow up, they are almost bound to be drawn into it, at least in the sense that their best friends will be other Sikhs, and most of their time and resources when they are not at work will be spent with their family or with Sikh friends.

Moreover, they are likely to become 'involved' in a more active sense in the corporate, political life of the community. This will be important; the community has agencies which have important functions in maintaining communal consciousness and furthering the mutual interests of its members, and which are, potentially at least, the best instruments for enabling the young British Sikhs to adjust to the life of the wider, Western society without sacrificing their pride in being what they are or being led to under-rate the contribution of their parents' culture and traditions.

There are deep-rooted traditions of participatory democracy amongst the Sikhs, organized in self-governing *Gurdwaras* with a central governing body in Amritsar elected through the *Gurdwaras*, the *Shiromani Gurdwara Parbandhak Committee*. In the course of religious celebrations in a *Gurdwara*, members of the community who aspire to 'leadership', and visiting preachers from elsewhere in Britain and from India, are expected to deliver sermons and these can impinge, through ethical and social matters, on politics. Like the chapels of South Wales, the *Gurdwaras* have fostered a tradition of political oratory. Temple politics can frequently become emotional and demagogic. In Britain, there are thrown together people who had some claim to importance when they were in the Punjab, with others who have achieved standing in the émigré community; there are people from many different villages and families, with loyalties, obligations and historic feuds to to prosecute; there are no generally accepted leaders, in the absence of any whose age and long service would entitle them to such respect. The result is constant factional and personal in-fighting of labyrinthine complexity. At the level of informal friendships and social contacts, there is the same complexity. In the Punjabi village, most of a family's friends and frequent visitors would be more or less distant relatives. In Britain, there are some families who only have close social contact with kinsfolk in the same town or further afield, but others have added Sikh workmates and neighbours to their circles of friends.

There are two possible reactions that might be expected amongst young people in a minority community who feel discontented with either the treatment they get when they attempt to become part of the 'host' community or with the constraints placed on them by their own community, or with both. They may associate themselves with other young people in the wider community who are, for one reason or another disaffected, and politically with movements aiming to reform the whole system, and incidentally to remove the injustices which they feel they are suffering; or they may identify themselves very strongly with the distinctive character of their own community, and within it with movements aiming to 'purify' it in some sense and to restore its pride in its distinctive identity.

Within the existing pattern of 'first-generation' Sikh immigrant politics, there are the beginnings of both such developments.[1]

The desire of Sikhs to identify themselves actively and positively with the distinctive *Khalsa Panth* and to participate in its communal life has encouraged the growth and success in the Punjab of the 'communal' party of the Sikhs, the *Shiromani Akali Dal*. The *Akali Dal* is a political party with militant origins dedicated primarily to the interest of the Sikh *Panth*, a kind of political party unfamiliar in England, but with parallels in Northern Ireland. It is prone to frequent internal disputes and breakaways, for *Akali* covers a wide range of political outlooks. In Britain, these fissiparous tendencies have been compounded by the conflicts of loyalty and leadership we have mentioned. There is a basic, running division in India and in Britain, between the 'peasants' and the 'intellectuals'; in the Punjab, the 'peasants' are typified by the dominating character of Sant Fateh Singh—dedicated, sometimes to the point of fanaticism, largely untouched by Western 'education', but capable of attracting the support of the great majority of *Jat* agriculturalists. The 'intellectuals' have greater claim to political expertise and the support of the educated middle classes, but have lost popular support by frequent, apparently unprincipled changes of policy and loyalty. This basic division in Britain is reflected in disagreements between older immigrants, those with some claim to respect in the community in India, conservative elements who dislike many aspects of life in Britain, and those, mostly rather younger, who have achieved standing in the community mainly by their knowledge of English and of the 'workings' of the British society. But the division is not simple—all sorts of personal and family disputes are involved; points of principle seem to be taken up largely as tactics, and enthusiasm for 'symbolic' observance of traditional rules—wearing of turbans and so on—is as likely to be found amongst the young as the old. Moreover, *Akali* activity in Britain is largely an extension of Punjabi politics. Fund-raising, meetings, visits by 'leaders' to Amritsar and so on relate very much to such 'Indian' issues as the status of Chandigarh and the future of the Punjab as a 'Sikh Homeland'. This is unfortunate: there is a pressing need for such an organization to devote its energies, and very large finances, to more constructive work than faction-fighting, and prestige projects, the building of expensive *Gurdwaras*, the entertainment of supposedly important members of the 'white' community, visits and petitions to ministers and M.P.s. The Sikh religion, if it is to have any future in Britain, needs to be made meaningful to young Sikhs; the Punjabi language needs to be taught effectively; more knowledgeable members of the community could give all kinds of help to parents and children to anticipate and help

[1] I was helped in preparing this account of communal politics by Dr. Duncan Scott of the Ethnic Relations Research Unit, Bristol University, who gave me access to his unpublished findings. The opinions, and any misunderstandings, are my own.

to resolve the tensions that are bound to develop. There are efforts being made in this direction, mainly by organizations that have dissociated themselves from all political activities—the Sikh Cultural Society in London, the Sikh Missionary Society in Gravesend, but they are always in danger of being drawn into the quagmire of communal politics and used by would-be 'leaders' as instruments for their political ambitions.

The alternative—association with reforming movements in the wider community, secular rejection of communal politics (though not necessarily rejection of the traditions of the community, and even of militant 'symbolic assertiveness')—is the policy of the Indian Workers' Association,[1] a national body with a long history, dating back to the 1930s when the I.W.A. began as a movement amongst the relatively few Indian merchants, students and other emigrants in Britain to support the Freedom Movement in India. Since the 1950s, it has been very largely a Punjabi (and so Sikh-dominated) organization, traditionally left-wing, sympathizing with the Congress and the various Communist parties in the Punjab, and with the Labour and Communist parties in Britain. It is, like the *Akali Dal*, subject to factionalism, which is made worse by the factionalism inherent in left-wing movements generally; thus, there are 'Stalinist', 'Trotskyite', 'Maoist' and 'Naxalite' labels attached to groups that are likely to originate in personal and family or village rivalries. However, the I.W.A. is probably better able to cope with the real problems that face Sikhs, for example in the work situation, through its links with the British trade unions via the Labour and Communist parties.

These political organizations are a part of the self-sufficient social organization of the community. They help settle disputes amongst Sikhs, avoiding recourse to courts, they provide opportunities for individuals to pursue their ambitions and aspirations to 'leadership', and they are an extension of Indian political life into Britain. In all these respects, they are very much a creation of the 'first generation'. 'Second generation' political activity is emerging only gradually; teenage boys who have spent an increasingly long time in Britain are participating more and more in these communal activities; if this continues, change could come from within, rather than taking the form of complete rejection by the creations of their elders. It is important to realize that these political organs—the 'communalist' *Akalis*, the 'radical' I.W.A.—are both potential instruments for the 'second generation' to use in efforts to effect changes both within the community and in their relations with the rest of society, not least as organizations to resist racial discrimination and to counter prejudice; in effect, the community has its own, inbuilt means of 'containing' youthful rebelliousness in the same way as it 'contains' its own internal dissensions.

[1] See De Witt John, *Indian Workers' Associations in Britain*. Bibliography, section 10.

8 The Future

At present, nearly all teenage Sikhs in Huddersfield are Indian-born, and most migrated when they were old enough to retain some memories of India. As time goes on, they will be outnumbered by those who came when they were infants, and those born in Britain. A steady, inexorable process of 'anglicization' might be expected amongst the rising generation: their elders certainly feel that this is happening, and are anxious and defensive as a result. They see their children 'growing away' from them; the re-learning, of language, customs and ways of thought necessary to keep pace with the younger generation is too much for them. Yet the whole logic of their own society demands that young people should try to fulfil the ambitions of their parents, that they should remain as 'branches' of the family economically, like branches of a business, that they should remain identifiable members of the Sikh community.

In the battle for these children's souls, the 'host community' has many advantages. Ironically, the more eager the Sikh parents are that their children should 'succeed'—on the parents' terms—the more they have to entrust the upbringing of the children to non-Sikh agencies, especially school, college and the place where they start work. The more progress that the young Sikh makes in the race for 'qualifications' and a job worthy of his abilities, the more he is influenced by Western values, especially the importance attached to individual initiative, the right of the individual to form his own opinions, and to question norms of belief, morality and social behaviour. Of course, many of the tensions within the Sikh community, especially tensions between young and old, are a product of the rapidly changing, complex and varied society in which we live. When we look at the difficulties of Sikh parents and children in an industrial town in Britain, we see a microcosm reflecting much wider conflicts and changes. First generation immigrant parents may not realize this, and see the issue as a straightforward tug-of-war between the immigrant community and the host society for the souls of the children.

There is the same 'communication gap' between young and old, too, but for the Punjabis it is aggravated by the fact that the language of home is totally different from that of school and work.

There is the idea inculcated at school—whether deliberately or not
—that it is 'wrong' to use Punjabi, that English has a 'superior'
status (just as English-speaking children may be taught that the
English of home is 'bad' English, while that of school is 'good').
For an increasing number of children, the mother-tongue is not an
adequate means of communication—they are simply not fluent in
Punjabi because English has played such an important role in
their lives since such an early age; so the conversations of their
parents and relatives, and all that appertains to their religion and
culture, are literally meaningless to them.

The older generation—and not just the older Sikh generation—
might wish that education was more 'formal', more a matter of
learning facts and passing exams rather than asking questions,
exploring and learning to criticize; they might wish that the media
purveyed a less ambivalent set of moral attitudes, that true and
false, right and wrong could be as clearly distinguishable as they
are in the tradition-bound environment of the village. But the
fundamental threat to the communalistic, closely-knit family and
social life that they are used to could not be removed even if Sikh
children were to be taught in the most rigidly formal manner,
thoroughly indoctrinated with Sikh religious teachings, and shielded
from the influence of television, advertising and the fashions of
other young people—the fact that cannot be wished away is that
young people can have economic independence. In the Punjab,
until recently, an individual who attempted to live on his own
resources, attempting to maintain a wife and children by his own
efforts, had little chance of surviving, and none of maintaining the
standard of living possible in a joint family household, with its
economic distribution of shared resources. Economic necessity was
the strongest link binding together the 'extended family'. For young
Sikhs in Britain there may still be economic advantages (considering the financial difficulties of young people trying to set up home
independently), but there is no such overriding necessity. If the
family's character is to survive at all, it can only be because everyone concerned agrees that it offers them some emotional or social
benefits, not because they would starve without it.

The desire for—and possibility of—economic independence may
bring to the surface all kinds of resentment that the closely-knit
family generates. The authority of a young father, away from home
all day or even evenings and nights is likely to be less than that
exercised by the aged paterfamilias in the Punjab, but young
people are still likely to resent what they see as attempts by their
elders to dominate their own lives. The inward-looking atmosphere
of family and community life may be stifling, with the feeling that
everybody is watching how everybody else behaves, everything
one does or says is scrutinized, and everyone is at the mercy of
gossip within the local community and, at long range, amongst

relations and family connections in the Punjab. Jealousy emerges —a boy envies an older brother who has 'broken free', as he sees it, or else suspects that he has been sent out to work so that younger brothers and sisters can have a better life than he has had. The most serious crises, as we have mentioned, are likely to be conflicts between parents and children—especially girls—over arranged marriages; for Sikh parents, willingness to accept arranged marriage is the ultimate test of the child's willingness to 'belong'. There is no sign that determination over this issue is weakening; if anything, the strength of other challenges to their way of life is so great in British society that Sikh parents have become more strict over this issue than they would be in India, where a 'love marriage', though very regrettable, might be less than a total disaster. On the other hand, as the present generation of girls grow up, and themselves have children, they may become an increasingly powerful force for change the influence of Western education and ways of behaviour sharpened by a determination not to inflict on their children what their parents imposed on them. The strength of this tendency will depend on the number who stay in Britain rather than returning to India to marry, and the reverse, the number of girls imported from India to marry 'British Sikh' boys.

While choice of a marriage partner is seen as the principal battle, other issues can provoke preparatory skirmishes—the wish of young people to go out at night with friends, especially friends of the opposite sex, their wish to spend their money on their own choice of fashionable clothes, their own tastes in entertainment, their own opinions about their careers, their own views on religious or political matters. It is wrong to pretend—as some apologists on both sides do—that there is no fundamental difference between the Sikh religion and way of life and the basic ideals and values of other traditions, notably Protestant Christianity. A tradition such as we have described, with its emphasis on *Dharam* and *Sewa* is in real conflict with a culture that places highest value on freedom, individual initiative, and privacy. Again, this conflict is not a straight one—Sikhs versus the rest—but one which is a feature of any modern society, an element in the life of all communities, large and small; however, it is a very real conflict, and one that cannot be easily resolved by wishful thinking. If the important teachings of the Sikh Gurus, their teaching about the nature of man, the purpose of life, moral duty and so on, rather than their teaching about what one should or should not wear, are not explained to the young people, the religion will seem to them a meaningless jumble of superstitious observances. If other creeds and moral codes are presented to them in school, through the media or by their non-Sikh friends, in a more intelligible and attractive manner, they may feel that their parents' religion has nothing to offer them —the wearing of long hair, turbans, bangles or *shalwar* just more

pointless impositions inflicted by an older generation desperately
frightened of 'losing' the children. The desire to follow the fashions
of their contemporaries—clean-shaven, smoking, the girls dressed
in skirts, eating hamburgers, dancing to pop music, even having
'love affairs' may not be as serious a threat to all they believe in
as the parents think, but they could themselves turn such things
into issues of principle, amounting to a choice between religions.
The young Sikh, with money of his own to spend may be most
strongly moved by a wish not to be different from his non-Sikh
contemporaries, but for the more serious-minded, the influences
are more than just the current fashions—such disaffected young
people are likely to listen to the rhetoric of political radicalism,
offering the attractive possibility of wiping the whole slate clean,
washing away both the conservatism of the older generation and
the unpleasant features of the 'host' community—racialism—at one
revolutionary stroke.

To the non-Sikh teacher, administrator or politician, the reasons
why young Sikhs should conform, to an increasing extent, to the
ways of the majority community, and reject the exclusive and
'divisive' habits of his or her parents, seem so good and so many
that it is regarded as a foregone conclusion that the second, and
certainly the third generation will move steadily, inevitably towards
total 'Westernization'. To many Sikh parents, too, the outside
influences on their children's behaviour seem so powerful that
they feel unable to counter their effect, and they are driven either
to resignation, accepting the 'Westernization' of their children as
inevitable, or to drastic measures such as sending them back to
India. We have summarized a few of the obvious economic,
emotional and social reasons why these points of view seem
plausible—the desire for, and possibility of economic independence,
the influence of western, 'liberal' education, resentment of parental
domination and the claustrophobic atmosphere of the joint family
and small community, desire to identify with their non-Sikh
contemporaries, and so on. The effects of these are obvious to
everyone concerned, but is this judgement rather superficial? Are
the changes in the behaviour of Sikhs in Britain more apparent
than real?

The first, fundamental influences on the character of the Sikh
child are not from the 'outside' western culture; they are the
influences of home—mother, father, sisters and brothers. The
greater part of our essay has concentrated, deliberately, on describing the nature of *these* influences. Our general impression is of
marked consistency and integrity, positive and responsible concern
on the part of the whole family for the welfare of the child and
the formation of his character. We have seen how the early life
of most of these children is highly favourable to the acquisition
of skills, manual and intellectual, and positive motivation to learn

and to enjoy success at school. But we have emphasized that this development is within a limited framework of assumptions—the accepted beliefs and moral standards of the family and the community are taken for granted, they are not objects for questioning or discussion. The ideal personality that the Sikh parents try to form in their children is conformist, loyal, co-operative, moderate in his demands and expectations, disciplined and self-disciplined. Their aims may be frustrated by all kinds of external factors and conflicting influences, but the first few years of life, and the influence of home and family may prove to be the most important.

This is especially likely in view of the fact that home provides such a stable, secure and happy environment for the young child. We have mentioned how the early life of Sikh children is spent in an atmosphere of closeness to and dependence on mother, and the many ways in which affection and loyalty for other members of the family is fostered. In later life, the family remains—for most young Sikhs—the only safe and secure 'anchorage'. To subject one's individual ambitions and desires to the wishes and interests of the family group may involve some swallowing of pride, even humiliation, but everything in the child's early life encourages him to expect and to want the emotional security that only the family can give. The family is itself subject to the scrutiny of a wider group, the Sikh community in the neighbourhood, and its 'branches' elsewhere, especially the family 'home' in the Punjab; the individual who accepts the protection and stability of the family is obliged to protect its good name by living up to the standard of the community. This applies especially to girls; we have seen how the home upbringing of Sikh girls is very largely preparation for marriage and motherhood, and we have tried to explore some of the conflicts that different ways of behaviour, different educational objectives and different moralities can create for the girls and their parents. The alternative—accept or sacrifice all your security and hope of a peaceful life—may seem like emotional blackmail, but it is a blackmail which the girls may be predisposed by their upbringing to accept. In spite of the strictness of what they say on the subject, there are signs that even first-generation parents are unwilling to go to the final extreme in forcing their wishes on an unwilling daughter—the stability of family life depends on compromise or give and take amongst family members, not an autocratic rule from the head of the family. If the marriage-system is maintained, with only gradual modification—for example, parents and children consulting each other on the choice of partner—and especially if the immigration of girls from India to marry boys here continues, a most important factor preserving the distinctiveness of the community (in its own eyes and the eyes of non-Sikhs) will survive.

The wish of teenagers to be like their contemporaries rather than toeing their parents' line, is bound to be a strong influence on their development in adolescence. But it is open to question just how strong an influence it can be, and whether it is likely to be sufficient to provoke a complete, irretrievable break with their families and community. As things are, there is little sign of a mixed 'Anglo-Asian' teenage culture developing (there is much more possibility of such an 'Anglo-Caribbean' development). Language can still be a barrier, even for the child who has been in Britain for many years, and who, for the purposes of school work and formal social relationships, can be regarded as fluent in English; it is the very specialized language of personal and group relationships which is so hard to learn.. Young teenagers need friends amongst their contemporaries in whom they can confide. Sikh children may find they have neither the common code of language nor the common background of experience that they need to form really satisfying relationships with other children at this age, and so, even children who have grown up in Britain and been through Infant and Junior schools in the company of non-Sikhs, when they come to adolescence, are likely to gravitate into an all-Sikh peer-group; there is both their own developing sense of 'belonging' to a distinctive group, and the sense of non-Sikhs that they don't 'belong' to their group.

It is at this stage that the insults, 'wog', 'pakky', which amongst younger children seemed no more than part of the common stock of playground epithets, along with 'fatty' and 'four-eyes', seem suddenly to become meaningful. Children aged 10 or 11 who had spent most of their childhood in Britain have told their parents or confided in me that the 'wanted to go to India'. Why? They had made this discovery that they were 'different' and that they were disliked and suspected for this reason. This is, for these children, a special, additional and quite shattering part of the dawning self-awareness of adolescence.

We have tried to describe sympathetically the pressure and tensions within the family and community that affect young Sikhs, as teachers and others concerned need to be aware of these, and it requires a certain degree of sympathetic imagination to understand them—but how much more difficult to imagine is the effect on a child's or young person's character of this constant, grinding sense of surrounding hostility. If we have suggested that the difficulties of young Sikhs are all generated within their own community, that they all derive from conservatism and over-anxiety on the part of the parents, this is a false impression. The fact of racial hostility is a part of their lives, a permanent backdrop to all the tensions and conflicts that we have examined in more detail.

Awareness may come with adolescence, but the reality of racial hostility is there from the start. Even children who are said to be too young to have 'prejudices' are not too young to suffer from discrimination. Children who have learnt English and spent much time with English-speaking children must be more conscious than their parents of the significance of the awkward silences, the hostile glances, the over-polite tones of voice and muttered comments that the appearance of a Sikh family can provoke in a shop, on a bus, or at a playground. They are not too young to be aware that their parents and the group they belong to is being abused, bullied and browbeaten. A sense of grievance can be very strong even when it cannot be expressed in words or action.

Many Sikh parents and children are becoming frustrated by failure in the education system. The stock answer is that their ambitions are 'unrealistic', but this is hardly fair to a child who is kept in a 'Special Class' ostensibly to learn English when he or she has been in Britain for years, or when he or she is moved out of the 'Special Class' into a bottom stream, euphemistically termed 'remedial' class with little hope of redemption, especially when such classes are physically separated from the proper school and are housed in condemned or all-equipped premises. Their self-confidence is not enhanced by curricula which ignore the achievements of all races of the world except whites, and all civilizations except Western Christianity. Even where arrangements are made that are intended to be beneficial to the child, 'positive discrimination', they do not always seem so to the parents, and the child, even at an early age, is well aware that he is being treated 'differently', and that his parents are not getting satisfaction when they query or object.

As they grow older, the young Sikhs' sense of alienation is reinforced by all kinds of incidents with their white contemporaries, and by encounters with hostility in adults—teachers, employers, the police—often unintentional or unconscious arrogance, rudeness or lack of respect, but also downright racialism. They become aware, too, and are constantly reminded by television and the press, that this hostility is being exploited by politicians, national and local. Inflammatory speeches, tendentious reporting, the activities in Huddersfield of the National Front, are taken very seriously by the people against whom they are directed; with such things going on, they can hardly be accused of being 'over-sensitive'. The Sikhs have enough experience of migration and of being a minority not to expect too much of their neighbours: they do not expect to be welcomed with open arms. The reaction of the first generation, as we described at the beginning, was to avoid situations where unpleasantness would be encountered, to take whatever jobs and houses were available and to depend on the family and self-contained community for company and security. The second generation, and the more ambitious of their elders, are often critical of this behaviour; they feel that their parents are deluding themselves or taking a line of least resistance.

Older teenagers often seem to come to terms with the situation through a kind of cynical bravado—when they talk about difficulties that they face, in education or work or relations with parents, racial hostility does not seem to figure very highly; their attitude to overt racialism is one of impatience and scorn. But behind this assumed unconcern is a way of thinking that has come to take hostility for granted, to expect that most white people will be unpleasant, awkward or stand-offish towards them, and that any dealings with authority, employers and the wider society will be made more difficult by this fact. All those aspects of their lives that we have examined—family relationships, home life, religion, communal activities, education—are lived in such a 'siege' atmosphere. An essential part of the consciousness of these young Sikhs is this awareness that, even if they have spent most or all of their lives in Britain, this is not a secure home, and that they must keep links with another, more stable 'home'.

In this case, the seemingly 'meaningless' religious observances of their parents might take on a special, emotional rather than religious significance for the children. Wearing the '5 Ks', participating in the activities of the *Gurdwara*, maintaining religious observances at home, become symbolic assertions of identification, a passport to the security offered by the *Khalsa*, making emotionally 'real' the assertion of Guru Gobind Singh that 'five Sikhs are the equal of a hundred and fifty thousand'. This team-spirit can be reinforced in many, secular ways—especially if the young people visit their relatives in India. It is strengthened by patriotic films at the Indian film club, by the songs and speeches on Republic Day and Independence Day, by keeping up with news from India, by supporting Indian cricket and hockey teams touring Britain. It is reinforced by the activities of both the 'communal' *Akalis* and 'nationalistic' Indian Workers' Association. The coldness and hostility of the '*gora*' (white man) is contrasted by the chumminess and hospitality amongst the Sikh community. The boy or girl who abandons all this has no guarantee that he or she will find any substitute for it, unless he or she is very fortunate in marriage.

Nor need this identification with the Sikh 'team spirit' mean complete submission to their parents. In fact, the all-Sikh peer group of teenage boys might be regarded by Sikh parents as a subversive threat, though it will reinforce the group-loyalty of their sons. One could even see Sikh youth 'outdoing' their parents in religious fanaticism; they might initiate a movement (like that of the young West Indian and African negroes associated with 'Black Power') to revive or 'purify' the Sikh religion. Wearing of turbans and beards could become an act of defiance not just against the hostile white community but against the more nervous or half-hearted older Sikhs.

In effect, the young Sikhs now growing up in Britain are complex personalities, moulded by a variety of conflicting influences, products of a rapidly changing and ambivalent situation. We have mentioned some of the powerful factors drawing them away from their own family roots and communal ways towards closer conformity to the ways of the community at large; we have described some of the countervailing forces, the ties and pressures that may keep them within their own community. But their situation is not even as straightforward as this; between the contradictory demands and pressures, the personality of the child is itself developing creatively, and he is unlikely to submerge his own identity entirely in either the family or the wider group. There is in this situation the danger of serious emotional disturbance—maladjustment, mental breakdown, and so on. The stability of the family offers some protection against this, and it is essential that teachers at all stages of their education should have understanding of the situation and sympathy (for the parents as well as for the children). But there is also the possibility of really positive, creative development *within* the Sikh community over two or three generations, change generated within the community, not forced on it by outside pressures. It would not be a matter of compromise, 'watering down' the traditions of the Sikhs to hide differences from Western ways of thought and behaviour. Within the teachings of the *Guru Granth Saheb*, there is—it seems to me—a central core which is different from the basic teachings of any other religion or sect, and markedly different from the Western, humanist-Christian view of reality and man. It is not just a product of a particular community living in a particular part of the world at a particular time, but a valid philosophy of life in a totally different setting. It would be tempting to describe in detail my own interpretation of this 'central core', and my own understanding of its validity in our world, but it is not for me to say how the young British Sikhs will interpret it. It is enough to declare my confidence in these young 'strangers', to plead for an effort of understanding, sympathy, and encouragement on the part of teachers and all who have to do with their education, in the belief that they may, like other minorities before them—the Quakers or the Jews, for example—make a contribution to the life and culture of our country out of all proportion to their numbers.

Bibliography

A selection of books that have influenced me directly or indirectly in writing this essay, and some which could be of use to teachers working with Sikh children.

Abbreviations

S.C. *The Sikh Courier*: this is the principal English-language publication of Sikhs in Britain, mainly dedicated to articles on religion. Published three or four times a year by Mrs. P. M. Wylam, 38 Gloucester Circus, London S.E.10. References in this bibliography to articles are identified by volume and issue number; certain books and pamphlets are also available from the same address; these are marked S.C. in the bibliography.

I.P.C. Independent Publishing Company, 38 Kennington Lane, London S.E.11 4LS; importers of books from India. Books marked I.P.C. in the bibliography are most easily available from this source.

S.M.S. The Sikh Missionary Society, 27 Pier Road, Gravesend; they publish a number of booklets about the Sikh religion for children and adults.

1. General Background on the Sikhs and the Punjab

Essential reading is:

KHUSHWANT SINGH, *History of the Sikhs.* Oxford University Press, Vol. 1, 1963, Vol. 2, 1966.

He has also written shorter books on the Sikhs, such as *The Sikhs Today*, Orient Longman, 1968.

For general accounts of India, mentioning the Sikhs in historical perspective:

NEHRU, J., *The Discovery of India.* Asia Publishing House, Bombay, 1961.

THAPAR, R., *History of India Vol. 1.* Penguin, 1966.

SPEAR, P., *History of India Vol. 2.* Penguin, 1965.

EDWARDES, M., *History of India.* Thames and Hudson, 1961.

MORAES, F., *India Today.* Macmillan, 1960.

Other useful general accounts of India:

LANNAY, R., *The Speaking Tree.* Oxford University Press, 1971.

KOSAMBI, D., *Culture and civilization of ancient India*. Routledge & Kegan Paul, 1965.

BETTELHEIM, B., *India Independent*. MacGibbon and Kee, 1968.

For geographical background:

SPATE, O. H. K., *India and Pakistan*. Methuen, 1957.

A critical account of writing about the Sikhs, which is also a useful bibliography for anyone wishing to read more deeply, is:

HARBANS SINGH, *Sikh Studies*. S.C., Vol. 5, No. 1, 1968.

The same writer has written a number of books on the Sikhs and their religion, notably:

Heritage of the Sikhs. Asia Publishing House, Bombay, 1964.

There are many books now available about the 'background' of immigrants in Britain, giving some attention to the Sikhs; many of these need to be regarded with caution—the accounts are often excessively brief and sketchy, and inclined to be misleading or quite inaccurate.

MORRISH, I., *Background of Immigrant Children*, University of London Press, 1971, is more painstaking than most, and contains useful bibliographies.

Filmstrips and slides about the Punjab and Indian village life are available from the Commonwealth Institute.

2. General Background for Children

Teachers looking for books about India to use in class will be greatly helped by:

HILL, J., *Books for Children: the Homelands of Immigrants in Britain*. Institute of Race Relations, 1971.

The only major omission from this useful critical bibliography are the delightful publications of the Children's Book Trust, New Delhi, which can be obtained from Oxfam Marketing Division, Banbury Road, Oxford. The general books about India for children that give the most accurate and favourable account, mentioning the Sikhs and the Punjab in context, are:

ZINKIN, T., *India and her Neighbours*. Oxford University Press, 1967.

THAPAR, R., *Introducing India*. Asia Publishing House, Bombay, 1966.

A book intended for teenagers, nicely illustrated but too brief to capture much interest, is:

MACLEOD, W. H., *The Sikhs of the Punjab*. Lyall Book Depot, Ludhiana, 1969.

COLE, W. O., *A Sikh Family in Britain*. Pergamon, 1973.

3. The Sikh Religion

There is no full account of the beliefs and practices of the Sikhs, so to understand the religion one has to rely on translations of *Gurbani* and historical accounts of the lives and teachings of the

Gurus to a considerable extent. Amongst translations, only one can be regarded as, in any sense, authoritative:

TRILOCHAN SINGH *et al.*, *Selections from the Sacred Writings of the Sikhs*. Allen and Unwin, for UNESCO, 1960.

This was the work of a committee of Sikh scholars, aided by the literary talents of Khushwant Singh; it is the source of most of the quotations from *Gurbani* in this essay (except where otherwise stated). This is, of course, only a limited selection; a complete translation on the same lines is proceeding.

Meanwhile,

MACAULIFFE, M. A., *The Sikh Religion*, Oxford, 1909, several reprints, remains the most readable, although modern Sikh scholars would disagree with some aspects. An account of Macauliffe's monumental labours is:

HARBANS SINGH, 'English Translation of the Sikh Scriptures'. S.C., Vol. 4, No. 4, 1967.

More recent translations of the complete *Guru Granth* suffer from the very great problems of interpreting abstruse and complex ideas into meaningful English without losing some of the original sense or imposing some individual interpretation; see:

KHUSHWANT SINGH, 'Problems of Translating Guru Nanak's Hymns'. S.C., Vol, 5, No. 5, 1970.

Those problems are compounded when translators make painful attempts to imitate the language of the Authorized Version of the Bible, e.g. Gopal Singh, *Sri Guru Granth Sahib, Translated into Free Verse*. I.P.C.

A *Granth Sahib* with word for word glosses in English, prepared by S.G.P.C. Amritsar is available from I.P.C.

A fair amount of literature in the way of booklets and devotional books in English is available from:

S.C., including *Rehat Maryada* (translation of the *rahat*, rules for personal observances, private and corporate prayer) and other pamphlets in Sikh observances and ceremonies.

S.M.S., including a series of booklets on the '5 Ks' (those on *Kesh* and *Kara* have been published).

I.P.C., who send catalogues on request, and from major *Gurdwaras* such as Leeds, Smethwick, Birmingham, Coventry, Gravesend, and Southall.

To books listed under 'General Background' (section 1, above) can be added:

WYLAM, P. M., *Brief Outline of the Sikh Faith*. S.C.

JAMES, A. G., 'Diwali at Amritsar'. *English for Immigrants*. Oxford University Press, Vol. 4, No. 2, 1971.

JOGINDER SINGH, *Sikh Ceremonies*. I.P.C.

HOLROYDE, P. *et al.*, *East Comes West*. Community Relations Commission, 1971.

This last is a 'background' book on the Hindu, Muslim and Sikh religions; its treatment of the Sikh religion is far from adequate. Studies of the Gurus include:

MACLEOD, W. H., *Guru Nanak and the Sikh Religion*. Oxford University Press, 1968.

TRILOCHAN SINGH, *Guru Nanak*. S.G.P.C., Delhi, 1971; I.P.C.

TRILOCHAN SINGH, *Guru Tegh Bahadur*. S.G.P.C., Delhi, 1967; I.P.C.

Guru Arjun. S.M.S.

NARAIN SINGH, *The Holy Guru Arjan*. I.P.C.

KARTAR SINGH, *Guru Gobind Singh*. 1932; reprint from I.P.C.

See also:

MACLEOD, W. H., 'The Janamsakhis of Guru Nanak'. S.C., Vol. 6, No. 1, 1970.

A filmstrip about the Sikh Religion is published by Concordia Films.

4. Books about the Sikh Gurus for Children

MALA SINGH, *The Story of Guru Nanak* is the most attractive. The S.M.S. is publishing a series of booklets for children aged about 9-13 covering the lives of all the Gurus; the three titles available at present are: *Guru Nanak*; *The Guru's Way*; *In the Guru's Footsteps*.

Available from S.C.:

WYLAM, P. M., *Guru Nanak*.

KAY, C. M., *A Story of Stories* (stories from World Religions).

5. 'Heretical' Sects

I know of books in English only from the *Radhasoami Satsang*, Dera Baba Jaimal Singh, Beas, Dist. Amritsar. This group seems most enthusiastic in attracting non-Sikhs, especially by appealing to the western interest in Yogic teachings:

MAHARAJ CHARAN SINGH, *Light on Sant Mat*. Beas, 1960.

MAHARAJ JAGAT SINGH, *Science of the Soul*. Beas, 1961

are amongst the more important publications.

6. The Punjabi Family

General accounts of Indian society:

ZINKIN, T., *Caste Today*. Oxford University Press for the Institute of Race Relations, 1962.

HUTTON, J. H., *Caste in India*. Oxford University Press, 1963.

DUBE, S. G., *Indian Village*. Routledge & Kegan Paul, 1955.

The Punjab in particular:

SMITH, M., in Srinivas, M. N. (ed.), *India's Villages*. Asia Publishing House, Bombay, 1960.

SMITH, M., 'The Misal: a structural village group'. *American Anthropologist*, 54, 1952.

A valuable account of aspects of the upbringing of children is:
BAIG, T. A., 'The child and mother-child relationship ... in India'.
Assignment Children 10, U.N.I.C.E.F., 1969.
On marriage, see:
'An Indian Girl Growing up in Britain'. *Multiracial School*, Oxford
University Press, Vol. 2, No. 2, 1973.
WYLAM, P. M., *The Sikh Marriage Ceremony*. S.C.
SIDHU, G. S., 'The Status of Women in Sikhism'. S.C., Vol. 4, No. 5,
1967.

7. Literature, Art and Music of the Punjab

For a general survey of Indian novels in English:
MUKHERJEE, M., *The Twice Born Fiction*. Heinemann, 1971.
DERRETT, M. E., *The Modern Indian Novel in English: a compara-
tive approach*. Editions de l'Institute de Sociologie de l'Université
Libre de Bruxelles, 1966.
An anthology of writing about India:
PANDEY, B. A., *A Book of India*. Collins, 1965.
The principal Punjabi novelists writing in English are Mulk Raj
Anand and Khushwant Singh. Books by Anand with Punjabi
background include his trilogy:
The Village. Kitub Popular, Bombay, 1939.
Across Black Waters. Kitub Popular, Bombay, 1940.
The Sword and the Sickle. Kitub Popular, Bombay, 1942.
The main novels of Khushwant Singh so far have been:
Train to Pakistan. Chatto & Windus, 1956.
I shall not hear the Nightingale. Calder, 1959.
A novel with a Hindu religious theme by a Punjabi writer is:
LALL, A., *Seasons of Jupiter*. Cape, 1958.
Articles on Indian writing in English will be found in the *Journal
of Commonwealth Literature*.
Unfortunately, there are not yet any translations of any major
Punjabi novels; a good anthology of modern short stories in trans-
lation is:
SINGH, K. and THADANI, J., *Land of Five Rivers*. Jaico, Bombay,
1968.
For Indian folk stories in general, see Janet Hill's bibliography
mentioned in section 2, above. Navrang of New Delhi is among the
Indian booksellers who would be able to supply books of folk
tales, etc.
Specifically Punjabi stories are not easy to find.
THAPAR, R., *Indian Tales*, Bell, 1961, includes *Sassi Pannu* and
some fables.
Heer Ranjha is in *Folk Tales of Pakistan*, available from Infor-
mation Department, High Commission of Pakistan.
On use of stories in school, see:

JAMES, A. G., 'Stories from the Punjab'. *English for Immigrants*, Oxford University Press, Vol. 2, No. 2, 1969.
For a sumptuous introduction to the painting of India in general, see:
RANDHAWA, M. S. and GALBRAITH, J. K., *Indian Painting*. Hamish Hamilton, 1969.
Another useful book on the subject is:
ROWLAND, B., *Art and architecture of India: Hindu, Buddhist, Jain*. Penguin, 1970.
ARCHER, W. G., *Paintings of the Sikhs*, H.M.S.O., 1966, is a magnicent monograph which, incidentally, brings to life the history of the Sikhs under Ranjit Singh and his successors.
On the leading Punjabi painter of the twentieth century:
DHINGRA, B., *Amrita Sher-Gil*. Lalit Kala Akademia, New Delhi, 1965.
Also a chapter in:
ARCHER, W. G., *India and Modern Art*. London, 1959.
The best introduction to Punjabi music—apart from hearing live performances—is through records. E.M.I. (India) have enfranchised distributors in towns throughout Britain where there are Indian communities; usually they are Indian shopkeepers, and they stock or can order records imported from India. Punjabi folk music has been recorded on a good series of L.P. records. *Folk Music of the Punjab*, ECLP 2253, is a good introduction, containing songs mentioned in this essay from *Heer Ranjha* and *Mirza Sahiban*; the popular singers Asa Singh Mastana and Surrinder Kaur have also recorded several E.P. records of folk songs (7/PE1866, 1867, etc.). Hindi film music is as ephemeral as any 'pop' music; distinctively 'Punjabi' music has accompanied films with a Punjabi background, such as *Shaheed*, *Nanak Nam Jahaz Hai* and *Heer Ranjha*. The Hindustani classical *Sangit*, recorded by such artists as Ravi Shankar and Vilayat Khan can be bought in many ordinary record shops. An interesting collection of actual field recordings of traditional music from different parts of India is Phillips BL7716 *Classical Ragas from India*—this is a good introduction to different instruments and modes of interpretation. See also KRISHNASWAMI, S., *Musical Instruments of India*, I.P.C.
There are several records of Sikh religious music available through distributors, including albums of *Asa di Var* and *Sukhmani Saheb* and E.P.s of selected *shabads*.
Accounts of Sikh religious music:
Sikh Sacred Music S.C.
CHAITANYA, K., 'Sikh Religious Music'. S.C., Vol. 6, No. 2, 1971.
There are also recordings of prayers, including an L.P. of *Japji Saheb* and *Rehiras*. All these are recorded by E.M.I. (India) and can be ordered through local distributors.

8. Punjabi Cookery

Nothing specifically 'Punjabi' in recipe books, but several books on Indian cookery by Sikhs. The most informative is SINGH, B., *Mrs. Balbir Singh's Indian Cookery*, Mills & Boon, 1961, with excellent introductions on ingredients and cooking techniques; the recipes include basic meat, bread, rice and sweet dishes as well as many more complicated things, but the treatment of vegetable and pulse dishes is rather limited. It can be augmented from DHARAMJIT SINGH, *Indian Cookery*, Penguin, 1970, but this is a collection of more elaborate recipes on the whole. I know of nothing, incidentally, on Punjabi handicrafts, dressmaking and so on; this is a pity. I am sure teachers, especially of Indian girls, would welcome some English accounts.

9. The Punjabi Language

The best introduction is:
GILL, H. S. and GLEASON, H. A., *A Start in Panjabi* (*sic*.). Hartford, Conn., Studies in Linguistics No. 2, 1963. This was written primarily for Peace Corps volunteers going to the Punjab (so is strong on the vocabulary of farming, shopping and school-teaching, but also gives much guidance about polite forms of expression, conversational idioms and so on). A useful companion volume is:
GILL, H. S. and GLEASON, H. A., *A Reference Grammar of Panjabi* (*sic*.). Hartford, Conn., Studies in Linguistics, No. 3, 1962; revised edition, Punjabi University Press, Patiala, 1969. The revised edition has an excellent chapter on Gurmukhi orthography; both the American editions use a phonetic roman script.
Much cheaper than these two, but also much less satisfactory is:
SHACKLE, C., *Teach Yourself Punjabi*. English Universities Press, 1972.
A short account of the Punjabi language, as an introduction:
SINGH, G., 'Punjabi and its Dialects'. S.C., Vol. 6, No. 2, 1971.

10. Sikh Migrants in Britain

For migration by Sikhs throughout the world, see the bibliography to Khushwant Singh's *History*. ... (Section 1, above).
Migration to Canada and the U.S.A. is very well documented, but little has been written about settlements elsewhere in the world.
On settlement in Britain, the classic is:
ROSE, E. J. B. *et al.*, *Colour and Citizenship*. Oxford University Press for the Institute of Race Relations, 1969.
On Sikhs in particular, see:
AURORA, G. S., *The New Frontiersmen*, Bombay, 1967; I.P.C. though this describes the situation in the 1950s only.

HIRO, D., *The Indian Family in Britain*, Community Relations Commission, 1967, is a 'background' booklet, too brief to be adequate. A realistic account of an Indian (Hindu) family's life in Britain is:

SHARMA, V., *Rampal and His Family*. Collins, 1971.

Migration into Huddersfield was recorded by:

GOODALL, J., 'Area Reports on boroughs with substantial immigrant settlements, 15'. Institute of Race Relations *Newsletter*, October 1966. (The information in chapter 1 of the present essay is from this source.)

Three important accounts of 'first generation' Sikhs in industry and politics sponsored by the Institute of Race Relations:

MARSH, P., *Anatomy of a Strike*. Institute of Race Relations, 1967.

JOHN, DE WITT, *Indian Workers' Associations in Britain*. Oxford University Press, 1969.

BEETHAM, D., *Transport and Turbans*. Oxford University Press, 1971.

See also:

DOVER, D., 'The Turban Problem'. Duplicated sheet circulated by the British Council of Churches, 10 Eaton Gate, London S.W.1.

11. Sikh Children in Britain

A general account of the response of education authorities to children of immigrants:

TOWNSEND, H. E. R., *Immigrant Pupils in England*. National Foundation for Education Research, 1971.

Two books describe the education of immigrant children in Huddersfield in the 1960s:

BURGIN, T. and EDSON, P., *Spring Grove*. Oxford University Press for the Institute of Race Relations, 1967.

SCOTT, R., *A Wedding Man is Nicer than Cats, Miss*. David and Charles, 1971.

Responses by teachers elsewhere are recorded in:

MCNEAL, J. and ROGERS, M., *The Multiracial School*. Penguin, 1971.

On infant children of immigrants:

DOSANJH, J. S., *Punjabi Immigrant Children*. University of Nottingham Institute of Education, 1967.

DERRICK, J., 'Listening to Language in the Infant School'. *English for Immigrants*, Oxford University Press, Vol. 4, No. 2, 1971.

GARVIE, E., 'Second Language Acquisition'. Ibid.

PEACE, W. M., 'A Study in Infant School Progress'. Ibid.

Immigrant Children in Infants Schools. Schools Council Working Paper No. 31, Evans/Methuen, 1970.

LUCAS, E., 'Language in the Infants Playground'. *Multiracial School*, Oxford University Press, Vol. 1, No. 3 and Vol. 2, No. 1, 1972.

A study of performance and potential of junior age Sikh children:

HAYNES, J., *Educational Assessment of Immigrant Pupils.* National Foundation for Educational Research, 1971.
This should be read in conjunction with:
Potential and Progress in a Second Culture. Education Survey 10, H.M.S.O., 1971. Also Miss Haynes' articles in *English for Immigrants.* Oxford University Press, Vol. 3, No. 1, 1969, and Vol. 4, No. 1, 1970.
On school-leavers and teenagers:
BEETHAM, D., *Immigrant School Leavers.* Institute of Race Relations, 1967.
'An Indian Girl Growing up in Britain.' See above, section 6.
JASBIR KAUR and KULWINDER KAUR, 'Young Sikh Girls in Britain'. Duplicated sheet circulated by the British Council of Churches, 10 Eaton Gate, London S.W.1.
THOMPSON, M., Abstract of paper to the British Association for the Advancement of Science, Swansea, 1971, describes his study of Sikh teenage boys in Coventry.
This is, of course, only a selection from the now extensive literature on the education of children of immigrants; see bibliographies available from: The National Association for Multiracial Education, 19 Margreave Road, Chaddesden, Derby.
The Community Relations Commission, 10/12 Russell Square, London W.C.1.
The journal *Multiracial School* published three times a year by the Oxford University Press.

Glossary

This lists the main references to the Punjabi words used in the text with a brief explanation of each one. In transcribing these I have followed the standardized spelling system now used in India for spelling place-names, etc. (except in the case of a few words—such as *ghee*, *purdah*—where an 'old-fashioned' spelling is already familiar in Britain). The spellings cannot give an accurate guide to pronunciation; several letters have to do duty for two or more Punjabi phonemes (e.g. the 'd' in *Akali Dal* is different from the 'd' in *dal* meaning 'pulse') and even if a complex system of diacritic symbols were used, it would be difficult to represent the differences in stress and intonation in words apparently similar (e.g. *ghòrá* and *gora*, *kirpán* and *kírtan*). Readers are therefore referred to the titles in the Bibliography, section 9.

Acchar, pickle, 40, 58

Adrak, root ginger, 57

Agarbatti, joss-stick, 34

Akali, Sikh militant, supporter of *Shiromani Akali Dal*, a Sikh communal political group; 'Saints' as leaders of, 42; blue turbans worn by, 48n; activity in Britain, 93-4, 102

Akand Path, complete reading of *Guru Granth*, 41

Alu, potato, 56

Amrit, 'Nectar', sweetened water used at *Pahal* ceremony, 47; the water in the artificial lake at Amritsar, 44; *Amritdhari*, baptized Sikh, 47-8

Anand Karaj, wedding ceremony, 86-7

Ardas, prayers used at the climax or end of religious ceremonies, 39, 48n

Arvi, root vegetable of yam family, similar to Jerusalem artichoke, 56

Atta, flour, 55n

Bala, infancy, 25

Bandgobi, cabbage, 56

Bante, marbles, 27

Barat, groom's friends and relations in wedding procession, 86

Bata, steel bowl used in *Pahal* ceremony, 48n

Bataon, aubergine, 56

Besan, gram flour, 58

Bhai, brother, any Sikh respected for piety and learning, the man entrusted with care of *Guru Granth Saheb* in a *Gurdwara*, 36

Bhangra, harvest celebration dance, Punjabi men's dance, 62-3

Bhindi, okra or lady's finger, a green vegetable, 56

Bhog, cremation, 45

Burfi, sweet made from dried milk, 57

Chaddar, shawl, blanket, 48; 'take under his *C.*', a man marries his dead brother's widow, becoming her protector, 16n

Chakri, ring of steel used as a weapon, a Sikh symbol, 32

Chapatti, unleavened bread, 25, 54-5

Chauri, fly-whisk, 38

Chuli, small clay oven enclosing a fire, used for frying or stewing, 54

Chuni, light silk scarf, worn usually by girls over their shoulders, 48

Dada, paternal grandfather, colloquially any elderly man, 83

Dal, pulse, 40, 56

Dalchini, cinnamon, 39

Dashera, 'Ten Nights', festival celebrating the battle of Sri Lanka and Sri Rama's victory, 42

Dehi, curds, yogurt, 40, 56

Desi, rustic, simple, ignorant, 64-5; *D. sharab*, home-made liquor, 59

Dhannia, coriander, 57

Dharam, duty, 24, 31, 40, 46, 77, 97; hospitality as, 40; food observances as, 54

Dharmsala, resting place for travellers, village meeting hall, 32

Dhola, side-drum, 38, 64; *Dholi, Dholak*, small, large forms of, 63-4

Dilwar, scimitar carried in Sikh religious processions, 32

Diwali, winter festival of light, new moon in month of Katak, 19n, 41-2, 59